BRIEFING NOTE ON CONVERSIONS

Use the following conversions as a guide to using the recipes in this book. Note that Australian tbsp measurements are larger than UK tbsp.

1 Australian tbsp = 20ml for four 5ml tbsp

1 cup water, stock, wine, soy sauce, mirin, dashi, etc = 250ml (8fl oz)

1 cup coconut milk = 250g (8oz)

1 cup plain flour = 120 g (4oz)

1 cup almonds, whole = 150g (5oz)

1 cup spring greens = 50g (2oz)

1 cup fresh herbs (basil, coriander, mint, tightly packed) = 50g (2oz)

NB It's always useful to have a set of measuring cups in the kitchen. These can be bought by mail order from Lakeland Limited, Alexandra Buildings, Windermere, Cumbria CA23 1BR telephone 01483 440 626 or Divertimenti, PO Box 6611, London SW15 2WG telephone 0181 246 4300.

Noodle

Terry Durack

Photography by Geoff Lung

PAVILION

Contents

Long life and happiness

To witness the birth of a noodle is a glorious thing.

I have listened, spellbound, as an 85-year-old noodle chef in Beijing told me why the act of making noodles helped him make sense of the world. As he spoke, he effortlessly stretched a soft, white blob of dough into a thick skipping-rope affair which began to dance before my eyes. It twirled and furled and stretched and strained until he deftly passed one end of the dough to his other hand, causing the rope to twist upon itself.

Back and forth he folded the rope upon itself until, for no reason apparent to mere earthlings, it split into noodles. A little twist, and it split into even finer noodles. And so it went, until the man had produced noodles so fine they could pass through the eye of a needle.

I have watched Mongolian noodle-makers slam their hand-pulled noodles so hard on their work tables that I feared the wood would splinter.

I have witnessed master soba chef Yoshi Shibazaki push and prod and roll his buckwheat dough until he was weak with the effort.

I have watched antique machines in outer suburbia steaming rough mixes of rice flour and water until they turned into a bridal white, gelatinous dough that was then stretched into shimmering silken sheets, cooled by rattly old fans hanging from the ceiling.

I have plunged my hands – well, my whole body – into flour in an effort to make my own noodles, ending up with a snow-white kitchen and a small bowl full of the most satisfying noodles in the world.

To all the people who create the noodles of the world, I dedicate this book.

I also make them a pledge: to treat their noodles with the same care, respect and integrity that they have shown by making them in the first place.

This is not a mere grab bag of quick-fix meals for the busy family on the run, even though many of the recipes can be done in a twinkle. There is no east meets west, no 'oriental pasta', and no garbage. Just great noodle recipes that I have cooked many times over in my long-suffering kitchen. They are recipes with roots; recipes with a tradition and a sense of history that reflect a region, a religion, a way of life, or a season.

Any modern recipes included are still firmly based in the framework of authenticity, and have been created by someone who loves, honours and respects the noodle.

Noodle survival

There are two ways you can use this book. You can start with a noodle, or you can start with a recipe.

Every noodle type comes with its own noodle i-d. Look up the i-d to find out what the noodle is, what it looks like, where it comes from, what it's made of, and how to cook it. At the end of every noodle i-d is a guide to recipes that use that particular noodle.

So if you find a pack of noodles in the cupboard and you don't know what to do with them, simply match them to a picture in the noodle i-d and check out the recipes that go with it.

If you already know what you want to cook, then simply look up the recipe, which will tell you the noodle you need. Check the noodle i-d before you go shopping, and you'll always cook with the right noodle.

A word on wok-cooking. Always heat your wok first, then add the oil, to prevent food from sticking. When the oil is smoking, add the food. For an authentic flavour, keep your heat up high. It helps to seal the food quickly, as well as imbuing it with the characteristic heat-seared flavour that the Chinese call 'the breath of the wok'.

As for stir-frying, you don't actually stir. Instead, you toss or flip. Use a paddle or broad spoon to get under the food, flick it up and toss it over onto itself, rather than stirring. Keep the noodles moving at all times, or they may stick, scorch or stew.

And never put too much in the wok at any one time. Unless you have industrial-strength heat and a giant wok, the noodles will sog before they can heat through. If you want to cook for more than four people, buy another wok and run two at once.

It's very, very difficult to undercook a noodle. It's very, very easy to overcook a noodle. When boiling or soaking your noodles to prepare them for cooking, keep them *al dente*, so they are still firm to the bite – especially if they are then going into a soup or stir-fry.

Above all, trust your instincts. If you want to add more garlic, add more garlic. If you want to leave out the chilli, leave out the chilli (but you'll go straight to hell when you die). Taste as you go. All you have to do is eat noodles, for long life and happiness.

Noodle i-d

1 Wheat
2 Egg
3 Hokkien
4 E-fu
5 Shanghai
6 Sevian
7 Fresh rice sheets
8 Rice vermicelli
9 Fresh round rice
10 Rice sticks
11 Bean thread vermicelli
12 Soba
13 Udon
14 Somen
15 Ramen
16 Harusame
17 Shirataki
18 Naeng myun
19 Dang myun
20 Gooksu

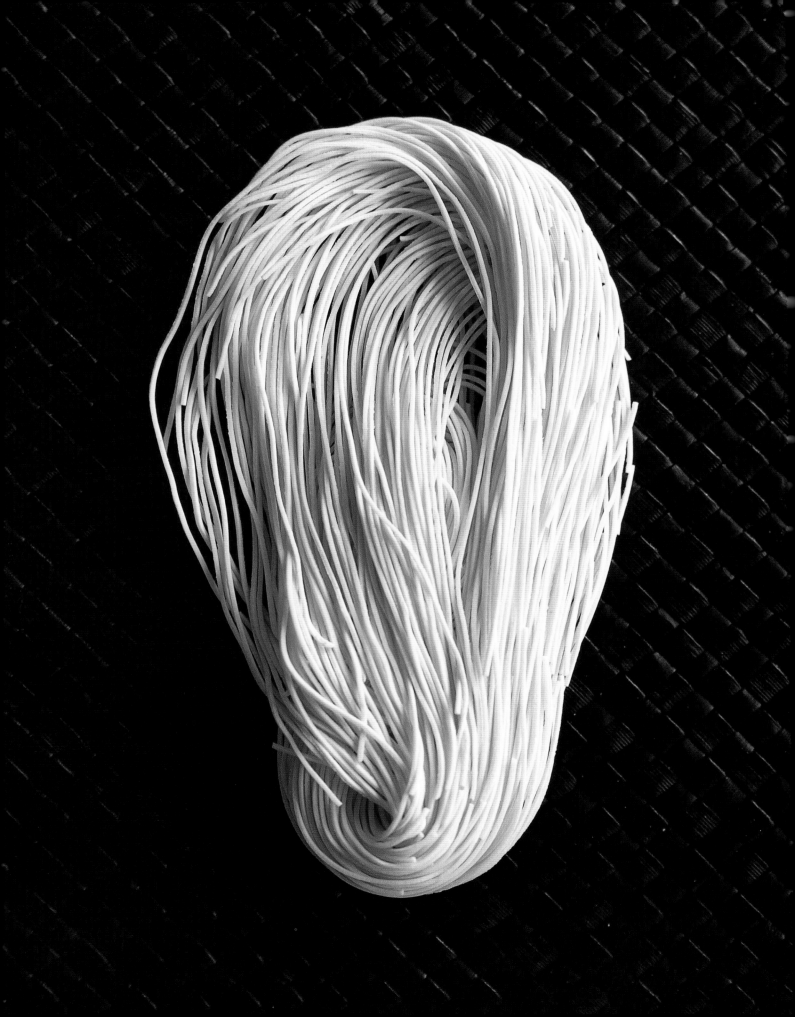

What

Meet the four-door family sedan of the noodle world. These thin, pale, eggless strands are go-anywhere, do-anything noodles, blessed with an inbuilt toughness and a heart of gold. Available in dried and fresh form, they are usually sold dried, even in China. If they had one home, it would be northern China, where most of them end their days in a happy stir fry. Wheat noodles are also available flavoured with prawn or crab, which sounds like a bad idea. Far better to add your own fresh prawn or crab.

Why

Because wheat noodles are the noble emperors of the stir fry. They work with all sorts of textures and flavours, soaking up juices like a sponge, and they're tough enough to withstand domestic abuse.

Where

Burma: kaukswe. China: gan mian (Mandarin) and kon mein (Cantonese). Japan: udon, somen and ramen are close cousins (see Noodle i-d 13, 14, and 15). Korea: gooksu. Malaysia: mee. Philippines: miswa. Thailand: mee. Vietnam: mi soi.

Which

Look for pale dried noodles sold either in rounds, like mini knitting yarns (shown), or in square blocks. Fresh wheat noodles are sold in plastic bags and should be kept in the refrigerator and used within a week of buying.

How

Dried: Cook in plenty of boiling water for about 4 minutes. Rinse in cold water, drain and reserve until needed.
Fresh: Cook in plenty of boiling water for about 2 minutes. Rinse in cold water, drain and reserve until needed.

Whatever

While egg noodles are more giving in texture and a little richer in flavour, they can nevertheless be substituted for wheat noodles. So if you're not sure whether your noodles are wheat or egg, don't worry about it too much: just keep cooking.

Recipes

Beef and water spinach noodles (page 54); Roast pork noodle soup (page 59); Two-sides-brown noodles with shredded duck (page 62); Eight treasure noodles (page 84–5).

Noodle i-d **2** Egg noodles

What

This is the closest any noodle gets to taking over the world. Seductive, slippery egg noodles stretch from one side of Asia to the other, and joyously cross the boundaries of breakfast, lunch and supper. It's the difference between fresh, silken tagliatelle made with eggs, and eggless spaghetti made with tough durum wheat. Made from wheat flour and egg, they come in various shapes and sizes (see also Noodle i-d 3 and 4), but here we want the classic thin, round variety to throw into soups, to stir fry, and even to deep fry. If you find thin flat egg noodles, either dried or fresh, save them for soups.

Why

Because they're instant texture food, mouth-filling and bouncy, with a satisfying chew. Because their slipperiness adds a new dimension to the humblest of bowling companions. And because they absorb whatever they are given, like an eager student, playing out the flavours of stocks and sauces with every mouthful.

Where

Burma: kyet-oo kaukswe. China: dan mian (Mandarin) and dan mein (Cantonese). Indonesia: bahmi. Philippines: pancit mami. Thailand and Malaysia: ba mee. Vietnam: mi.

Which

Dried: Look for nest-like bundles of golden noodles (shown). Any picture of a hen is a dead giveaway. *Fresh:* Check the refrigerated cabinet for plastic bags of sun-tanned golden noodles. These will keep for no longer than a week.

How

Dried: Cook in plenty of boiling water for 3 to 4 minutes, or until tender. Drain and rinse under cold running water; drain well. Set aside, covered, until needed. *Fresh:* Cook in plenty of boiling water for a minute. Drain and rinse under cold running water; drain well. Set aside, covered, until needed. Alternatively, fresh egg noodles can be deep fried, puffing up into crisp, golden beauties.

Whatever

Don't overcook. You will probably be cooking them again in a stir fry, braise or soup, so go for an 'al dente' bounce rather than an 'al denture' glug. If pre-cooking, add a little oil to avoid sticking.

Recipes

Eggflower noodle soup (page 50); Chiu Chow dessert noodles (page 51); Chicken chow mein (page 55); Chicken noodle soup (page 56); Wonton soup with noodles (page 61); Buddhist vegetable noodles (page 63); Cold noodles with spicy Sichuan sauce (page 72); Dan dan mian (page 73); Sichuan beef noodle soup (page 75); Sichuan fish noodles (page 76–7); Cross the bridge noodles (page 78); Dry-cooked green beans with noodles (page 81); Kao soi (page 133); Bahmi goreng (page 171); Panthe kaukswe (page 175).

What
Goodbye spaghetti, hello thick, fresh, oiled Hokkien egg noodles. Starring in quick, easy stir fries all over the globe, they originally started life as a favourite of the Hokkien Chinese, who in turn introduced them to Malaysia where they play a major role in Malaysian hawker-style dishes, such as Hokkien mee, mee rebus and mee goreng.

Why
Because of their satisfying, almost meaty bite. By virtue of their size, they take on more sauce and deliver more flavour, so choose Hokkien for all your saucy dishes.

Where
Although Hokkien noodles travel the world on a Malaysian passport, they are very big in China, where they are often substituted for the thick, white Shanghai noodle. They are also good substitutes for the increasingly rare hand-thrown Peking noodles in many dishes from northern China.

Which
Sold fresh or vacuum-packed in plastic bags, in the refrigerated section of Asian food stores and supermarkets. That sunny egg-yolk colour, by the way, is probably due more to food dye than sunny egg yolk, so avoid the overly bright ones. Choose loose-packed over vacuum-packed, because they are likely to be fresher, although they won't keep as long.

How
Place in a heatproof bowl and cover with boiling water for 30 seconds to 1 minute. Drain well, and use for stir fries and soups.

Whatever
Once the preserve of specialist Asian food stores, Hokkien noodles now pop up in suburban supermarkets. However, the noodles available in an Asian specialty food store can be superior to the more commercial brands carried by supermarkets.

Recipes
Hokkien noodles with prawns (page 67); Sichuan noodle-shop noodles (page 74); Noodles with pork and pickles (page 83); Curry mee (page 116); Hokkien mee (page 117); Indian mee goreng (page 118); Mee rebus (page 119); Laksa lemak (page 122–3); Penang laksa (page 121); Chilli prawn noodles (page 125).

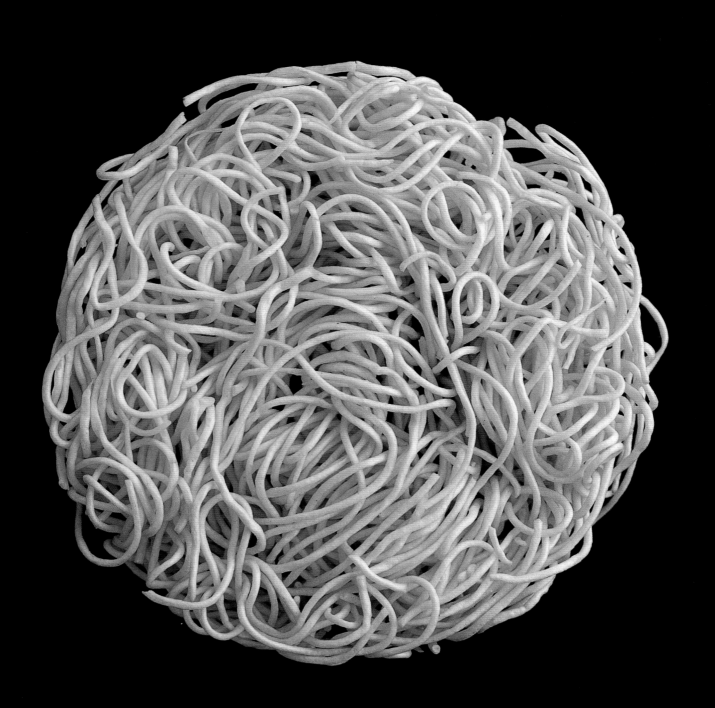

Noodle i-d 4 E-fu noodles

What
Birthday noodles. These thick, pre-cooked, deep-fried nests of e-fu noodles are a must at birthdays, family celebrations and Chinese New Year banquets because of their generous length. The longer the noodle you eat, the longer your life will be, and the more good fortune with which you will be blessed – hence the e-fu noodle's alias, long-life noodle.

Why
So you can live longer, of course. Not only that, but every extra meal in your longer life is made more enjoyable by the resilient, sturdy chew that comes from the double-cooking process.

Where
China: e-fu (Cantonese) and shi dan mian (Mandarin).
Philippines: pancit canton.

Which
You can't miss 'em. They look like crisp TV snacks that come in large rounds of golden, tangled, swollen noodles, in very large plastic bags. Often, you will find these bags hanging, rather than on a shelf in your Asian supermarket, as the noodle cakes are quite delicate. Carry home carefully.

How
Weirdly, you need to boil them for 2 to 3 minutes in plenty of water at a rolling boil to soften them, even though they have already been boiled and fried.

Whatever
Don't cut them. That would be seen as deliberately cutting years off the life of the person who eats them, who could be you. The longer, the better.

Recipes
Long-life noodles (page 58); Pancit canton (page 173).

What

Big worm-like noodles that are similar to Hokkien noodles, but in a raw state. Shanghai noodles are paler in colour, and are generally sold fresh, uncooked and unoiled. They are the traditional choice for serving with the famous pork and brown bean sauce the Chinese love as much as the Western world loves spaghetti Bolognese. They are also happy in soups and stir fries. Shanghai noodles work well in any dish that calls for hand-thrown Peking noodles.

Why

Because they are good solid, workmanlike noodles that slurp up soups and sauces with a desert island thirst. Because they're a particularly good alternative to the oiled Hokkien noodles when using sauces that are already quite oily.

Where

Northern and eastern China. Naturally, they are very big around Shanghai.

Which

Fresh Shanghai noodles come in plastic bags and are kept in the refrigerated section of Chinese food stores and supermarkets. They are pale, soft, and slightly dusty with flour, and have none of the sheen you see on Hokkien noodles.

How

Boil fresh, raw noodles in plenty of water for 4 to 5 minutes. Drain and rinse well in cold water, then set aside, covered, until needed.

Whatever

There is also a thin, pale wheat noodle (mian xian) that is sometimes referred to as a Shanghai noodle, but most Chinese cookbooks and chefs mean the thicker, more substantial variety when they specify Shanghai noodles.

Recipes

Brown sauce noodles (Zha jiang mian) (page 48–9); Stir-fried Shanghai noodles (page 70); Gung Bao chicken with Shanghai noodles (page 82).

Noodle i-d **6** Sevian

What
Nobody quite knows how an Italian-style fine vermicelli noodle found its way to India, but nobody is complaining, either. Finer than angel hair pasta, sevian – also called sev – is enjoyed throughout India in a milk pudding known as sevian kheer. It is also sometimes used in soups.

Why
Because these noodles have a pleasant fresh bread smell and a good, discernible taste that becomes even more pronounced when fried in ghee. But mainly because of the way they feel in your mouth, brushing it gently like the bristles of a soft shaving brush.

Where
They are a big favourite of Muslim people, so are found in Sri Lanka, Pakistan and Malaysia, as well as throughout the length and breadth of India.

Which
Sevian is always sold dried, normally in protective cardboard boxes, for it is extremely brittle, and is hard to handle without causing untold damage. It is usually a pale creamy colour, although there is a roasted variety that is a distinctive light brown.

How
Generally, sevian is eaten as sevian kheer, and needs only to be boiled in milk along with the other ingredients for about 15 minutes, so it absorbs some of the milk and flavourings (see recipe, page 181).

Whatever
For an impressive presentation of sevian kheer, add fresh rose petals, or a sheet of edible silver or gold leaf, available from Indian food specialists, just before serving.

Recipes
Sevian kheer (page 181).

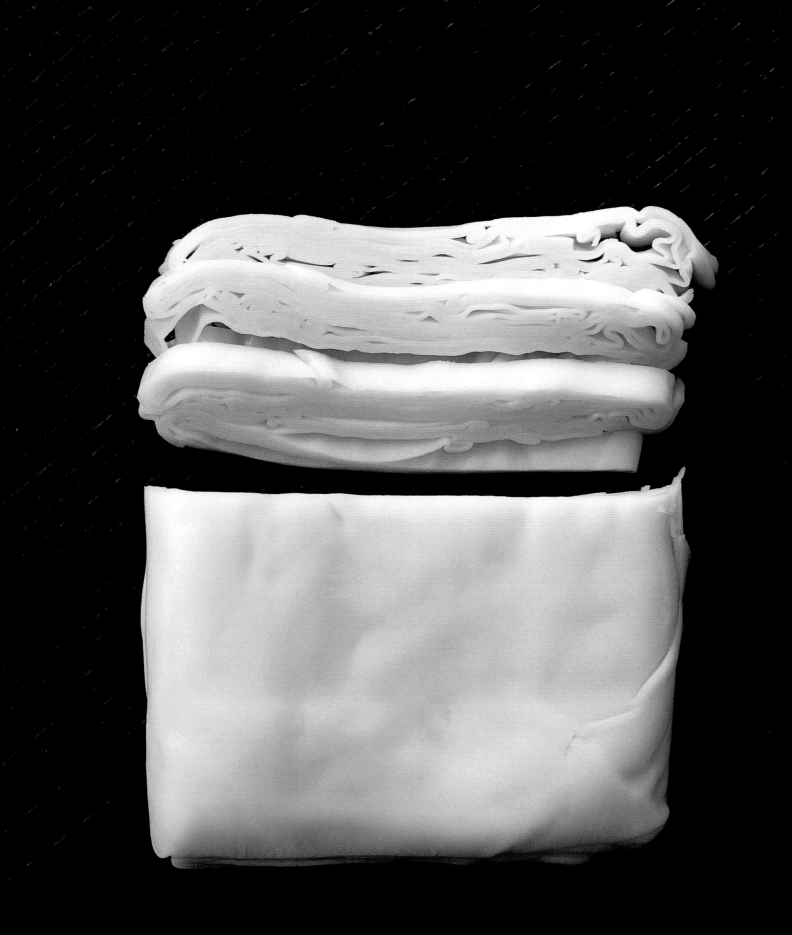

Noodle i.d 7 Fresh rice sheet noodles

What

These fresh, white, satiny noodles, cut into ribbons from fresh rice sheets, are delivered fresh daily to Asian food stores and supermarkets. Cantonese feast on them wok-tossed with thinly sliced beef, bean sprouts and soy. Thai people eat them as a lunchtime snack, teamed with beef, curry, pork or fish balls. Vietnamese devour them for breakfast as pho bo, a fragrant soup alive with noodles and beefy bits. Laotians also eat them in soup, flavoured with pork, garlic and a number of herbs, including the leaves of the marijuana plant. Malaysians eat them lightly scorched with the 'breath of the wok' in a slippery stir fry known as as char kueh teow.

Why

Because they are so flamboyantly voluptuous, angelically white, and refreshingly fresh, with a silken, slippery quality no dried noodle could ever hope to match.

Where

China: he fen (Mandarin) and hor fun (Cantonese). Malaysia: kueh teow. Thailand and Laos: sen yai or gueyteow. Vietnam: pho. Other: river rice noodles.

Which

Although flat rice noodles are also available in dried form, they really fulfil their silky promise only when fresh. Look for square plastic packs of noodle slabs that look like folded white satin pillowcases. These can then be cut into the desired noodle widths. Pre-cut fresh rice noodles are also widely available.

How

Just slice them into flat noodles of the required width, and pour boiling water on to cover. Gently pull the strips apart with a pair of chopsticks, drain and rinse, and they are ready to toss through a stir fry or slip into a soup.

Whatever

In spite of the notice on the pack to 'keep refrigerated', you will probably find them stacked beside, rather than in, the refrigerated cabinet. The truth is they will never taste as good as the day they were made, and while they will keep in the fridge for some time, they will almost instantly lose their generous supple texture, and break up when cooked. Fresh is best.

Recipes

Hor fun soup noodles with roast duck (page 52–3); Fried hor fun with beef (page 57); Char kueh teow (page 114–15); Gwaytio neua sap (page 132); Pho bo (page 152); Pho ga (page 153).

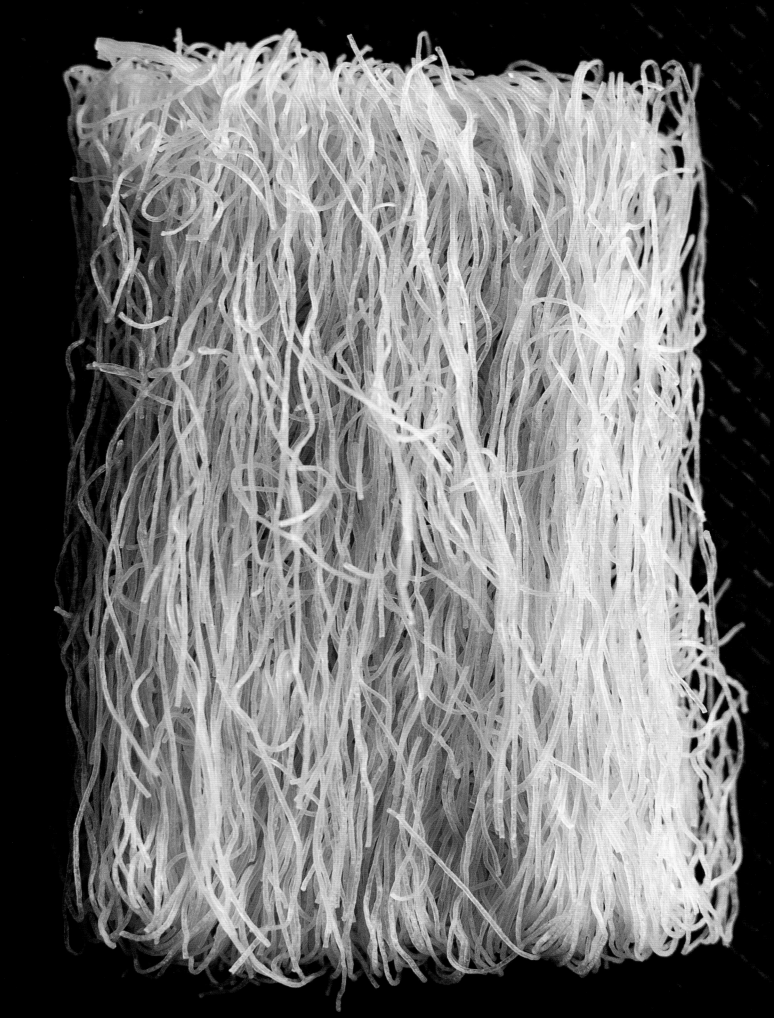

Noodle i-d 8 Rice vermicelli

What
The world's most versatile noodles. Throughout Asia, dried rice vermicelli pop up in spring rolls, slither into soups, find their way into a million stir fries, and puff up dramatically when deep fried. Known as rice stick noodles in China, these thin, dried, brittle white noodles are made from extruded rice flour paste. In Southern China, they are often matched with the local seafood.

Why
Because they give texture and contrast to a dish without adding too much bulk. Their neutral, almost bland taste makes them the perfect foil for curries and strongly flavoured dishes.

Where
Burma: hsan kyasan. China: mi fen (Mandarin) and mai fun (Cantonese). Malaysia: beehoon. Philippines: pancit bihoon. Thailand: sen mee. Vietnam: bahn hoi (an even finer rice vermicelli, used to accompany grills). Other: rice stick noodles (China).

Which
Rice vermicelli are usually sold dried in large bundles wrapped in cellophane. Semi-transparent when dried, they turn white with cooking.

How
For use in stir fries, pour on boiling water to cover and soak for 6 to 7 minutes, or soak in cold water for about 25 minutes. Rinse in cold water and drain. For salads, pour on boiling water and soak for 6 to 7 minutes. Transfer to a saucepan and boil for one more minute. Rinse in cold water and drain. For soups, cook noodles directly in plenty of water at a rolling boil for about 2 minutes. Rinse in cold water and drain. To deep fry, place dried noodles straight into the oil from the packet. They will puff up in much the same manner as prawn crackers, swelling to roughly four times their original size as if by magic.

Whatever
Don't get lost in the translations. While the Chinese call rice vermicelli 'rice sticks', Thai and Vietnamese rice sticks are different again (see Noodle i-d 10).

Recipes
Shanghai pork noodles (page 68–9); Chicken noodle salad (page 80); Hokkien mee (page 117); Mee Siam (page 120); Laksa lemak (page 122–3); Singapore beehoon (page 124); Mee krob (page 130–1); Moo sarong (page 135); Thai chicken noodle soup (page 142); Goi cuon (fresh spring rolls) (page 151); Nem nuong (page 154–5); Soto ayam (page 172); Mohinga (page 174); Stir-fried pumpkin with rice vermicelli (page 176–7); Khao pun nam ya (page 178).

Noodle i-d 9 Fresh round rice noodles

What
Delicate, fresh rice noodles that run from thin varieties, such as the Thai khanom jeen, to the thicker type that look like Hokkien noodles without the fake tan. Pale and interesting, they have made their presence felt throughout Southeast Asia, but most particularly in Malaysia, where they perform a public service in the famous laksa lemak and Penang laksa, and in Northern Vietnam, where bun noodles feature in a huge range of dishes.

Why
Because this is a truly unique noodle experience, combining the delicate flavour and sublime smoothness of rice vermicelli with the satisfying mouth feel and presence of a thicker noodle.

Where
China: lai fen. Malaysia: laksa. Philippines: pancit lug lug.
Thailand: khanom jeen. Vietnam: bun.

Which
Fresh round rice noodles are generally sold in a variety of thicknesses in plastic-wrapped trays. They will keep at room temperature for two days, or in the fridge for a week, but the quality deteriorates rapidly without refrigeration.

How
Pour boiling water over fresh noodles in a bowl, separating the strands gently, but quickly, with chopsticks, and being careful not to damage the noodles as you go. Drain, and refresh in cold water.

Whatever
If you have no luck finding fresh round rice noodles, the thicker variety can be replaced with Hokkien egg noodles (see Noodle i-d 3), while the thinner version can be replaced with rice vermicelli or thin rice sticks (see Noodle i-d 8 or 10). Dried khanom jeen can be found in Thai groceries, but they are a poor substitute for fresh. Malaysian restaurants outside Malaysia often serve both Hokkien noodles and rice vermicelli in their laksa soups, instead of the white laksa noodle.

Recipes
Penang laksa (page 121); Laksa lemak (page 122–3); Khanom jeen with spicy pork (page 134); Chilli mussels with rice noodles (page 140); Thai chicken noodle soup (page 142); Bun rieu noodle soup with crab dumplings (page 146–7); Bun bo Hué (page 148); Khao pun nam ya (page 178).

Noodle i·d 10 Rice sticks

What
These dried, translucent noodles act like rice vermicelli that have left home, seen the world, and grown up a bit. They are broader and thicker than rice vermicelli, running from slender sticks to the popular medium-width noodle, resembling pale tagliatelle. They are particularly popular in Vietnam, where they are often substituted for fresh rice sheet noodles, and in Thailand, where they are the main attraction of perhaps the most popular Thai noodle dish of all – the mighty pad Thai.

Why
Because they are tougher than fresh rice noodles, even after being boiled, and can handle the rough and tumble of the stir fry, as well as taking it easy in soups. They have more elasticity than fresh rice noodles, which gives them more bounce.

Where
China: gan he fen (Mandarin) and gan hor fun (Cantonese).
Thailand: sen lek or jantaboon.
Vietnam: hu tieu or Mekong rice sticks (containing tapioca flour).

How
Depending on their size, rice sticks should be boiled for 3 to 5 minutes. Or they can be soaked in warm water for 15 to 20 minutes.

Whatever
Choose your preparation method according to the dish you are cooking. If it is important that the noodles remain rigorously al dente, soaking is the best method. If you're looking for a more slippery, giving texture, boiling is the answer.

Recipes
Pad Thai (page 136); Pork and rice stick noodle soup (page 179).

Noodle i-d 11   Bean thread vermicelli

What
This noodle has more aliases than the Jackal. Referred to as bean thread, green bean thread, cellophane, jelly, transparent, glass, silver, and even invisible noodles, these thin, opaque white threads are made from an extrusion of mung bean starch and tapioca starch mixed with water. When soaked, they become gelatinous in texture and quite see-through. Their ability to absorb stock makes them ideal for soups, stews and soupy, braised dishes. They can even be deep fried, instantly expanding before your eyes in much the same way as rice vermicelli. They are also popular in desserts, enriched with palm sugar and coconut milk.

Why
Because they wiggle in the mouth, slipping over the tongue with divine lightness; because they look so good (fashionably transparent); and because they're fun to cook with.

Where
Burma: pekyasan.
China: fen si (Mandarin) and fun see (Cantonese). Malaysia: soo hoon or tung hoon.
Philippines: sontanghon. Thailand: woon sen. Vietnam: bun tau.
Other: Their close cousins, Japan's harusame (see Noodle i-d 16) is made from rice or potato flour, and Korea's naeng myun and dang myun
(see Noodle i-d 18 and 19), are both based on a combination of starches.

Which
Bean thread vermicelli are sold in tight white bundles that resemble rough, wiry, white knitting yarn. The most popular size packs are 250 g (8 oz), although they are also available in handy 100 g (3 oz) snack packs.

How
Pour boiling water over them in a heatproof bowl and let stand for 3 to 4 minutes. Rinse under cold water and drain. If deep frying, use straight from the pack.

Whatever
A pair of scissors is a must. These noodles are practically impossible to break by hand when dry, and can be quite a handful even after soaking, because of their length and propensity to tangle. A few strategic snips here and there will do the trick. When separating the strands for frying, work inside a large plastic or paper bag or you'll find noodles in strange places for months after.

Recipes
Noodles with shredded lamb (page 64–5); Lion's head meatballs (page 66); Ants climbing trees (page 71); Bang bang chicken noodles (page 79); San choy bau with cellophane noodles (page 86); Suckling pig, jellyfish and noodle salad (page 87); Seafood and glass noodle salad (page 137); Pad woon sen (page 138–9); Glass noodle som tum (page 141); Beef and glass noodle salad (page 143); Cellophane noodles with prawns (page 149); Cha gio (finger-size spring rolls) (page 150); Chap chae (page 158–9).

Noodle i-d 12 Soba

What
One of the world's truly great noodle varieties, soba are rugged, tough, protein-rich and extremely versatile. A lightly flecked, humble mushroom-brown colour, they are generally made from a combination of buckwheat and wheat flour, although some exclusively buckwheat flour soba are available. They are usually eaten in soup, or chilled with a dipping sauce. In Tokyo, they represent the epitome of noodle élan.

Why
Because they taste just as good hot or cold. Because they have a distinctive nutty flavour that makes them work even when served on their own with a dipping sauce of dashi, soy and mirin. And because they are high in protein, rutin and vitamins E and C.

Where
Although soba originated in the colder climes of northern Japan, they are equally popular in Tokyo. A distant relative, the naeng myun (see Noodle i-d 18), is also revered in Korea, where it is used in much the same way.

Which
Soba are usually sold dried in slim, elegant packets (shown), although some specialist Japanese shops may carry the freshly made variety.

How
Fresh soba: Drop into a pot of boiling water and cook for 2 to 3 minutes, or until al dente.

Dried soba: Bring water to the boil, add soba and when water returns to the boil, add 2 cups of cold water. When water again returns to the boil, add another cup of cold water. Repeat the process another 2 to 4 times, depending on the thickness of the soba, until the noodle is cooked but still resilient. Drain, rinse in cold water and set aside for use.

Whatever
A variation on the theme is the pretty green cha soba, made with the addition of matcha green tea powder. These noodles are more likely to be eaten cold than hot.

Recipes
Zaru soba (page 100–1); Tempura soba (page 103); Soba with eggplant and miso (page 110).

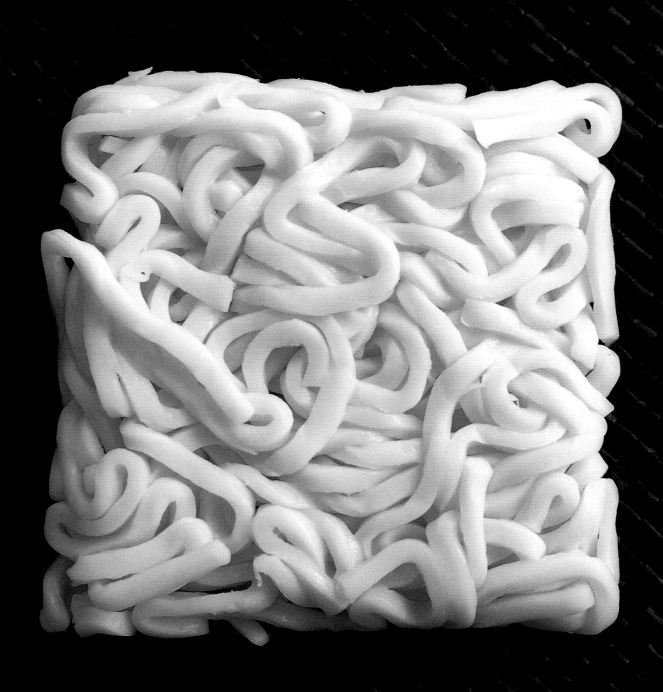

What

If soba (see Noodle i-d 12) represent Japanese noodle nobility, then udon are working man's heroes – large, white country-bumpkin noodles with a simple disposition and a generous nature. Can there be a more satisfying noodle in the world than these fat, glossy beauties? Their spiritual home is in the Province of Kagawa on the southernmost island of Shikoku, where official Udon Day is celebrated every year on July 2. Traditionally, these noodles are added to soup, but they can also be served cold and in braised dishes.

Why

Because they are completely satisfying noodles, with ample girth and slippery texture. And because the world would be a poorer place without a bowl of nabeyaki udon on a cold winter's day.

Where

Udon are generally associated with Osaka and the south of Japan, as opposed to soba, which are generally aligned with Tokyo and the north.

Which

Fresh or fresh/frozen udon are usually bulky, square-cut affairs, while the dried variety can be flat, square or round. Instant, pre-cooked udon are also sold in small square shrink-wrap packs (shown).

How

Dried: Place in a pot of boiling water. When water comes back to the boil, add a cup of cold water. When water again comes to the boil, add another cup of cold water. Repeat the process another 2 to 4 times, depending on the thickness of the udon, until the noodle is cooked but still has a little resilience. Drain, rinse in cold water and set aside.

Fresh: Place in boiling water and cook for 3 to 4 minutes. Drain, rinse in cold water, drain again and set aside.

Shrink-wrapped instant udon: Pour boiling water on top, and gently separate noodles with chopsticks. Drain, rinse in cold water, drain again and set aside.

Whatever

You must slurp your udon. In Japan, slurping noodles of any kind is mandatory, but particularly udon. Because of their generous size and solid nature, they tend to hold the heat longer, and are more urgently in need of a cooling intake of air with every single slurp.

Recipes

Curry udon (page 95); Memories of Shikoku udon (page 96–7); Fox noodles with chicken and mushrooms (page 98); Nabeyaki udon (page 99); Odamaki mushi (page 106); Moon-viewing noodles (page 108); Teriyaki salmon with udon and spinach (page 109).

Noodle i-d **14** Somen

What
Elegantly thin white noodles made from a hard wheat dough moistened with sesame seed or cottonseed oil. They are traditionally eaten cold, although they are sometimes served in a warm broth. This is the supermodel version of udon (see Noodle i-d 13), its country cousin.

Why
Because of their finesse and charm. Here is a noodle that dances on the tongue like a light shower, barely there, with a haunting, teasing texture.

Where
Philippines: miswa. Malaysia: bamee. Other: Japanese somen are also extremely popular in Korea, where they are often used as a foil for spicy, mouth-searing sauces.

Which
If you're lucky, you may find fresh somen, but the dried variety is far more common, and very handy to have in the cupboard. It is sold in packs – often very beautiful – of individual 'logs' of noodles, each tied with a little band. There are also three colourful variations:
Cha somen: green, from the addition of green tea powder
Tamago somen: yellow, from the addition of egg yolk
Ume somen: pink, from the addition of plum and shiso oil.

How
Dried: Put somen in a pot of boiling water and when water returns to the boil, add ½ cup cold water. When it returns to the boil, add another ½ cup cold water. After about 2 minutes, the noodles should be cooked. Rinse well under cold water, drain and set aside.

Whatever
For dramatic effect, Japanese chefs tie the end of a somen bundle together with string at one end before cooking. When cooked and chilled, swirl them artistically into the bowl and snip off the string.

Recipes
Chilled somen (page 94); Somen with salt-grilled snapper (page 104–5); Spicy squid with somen (page 165).

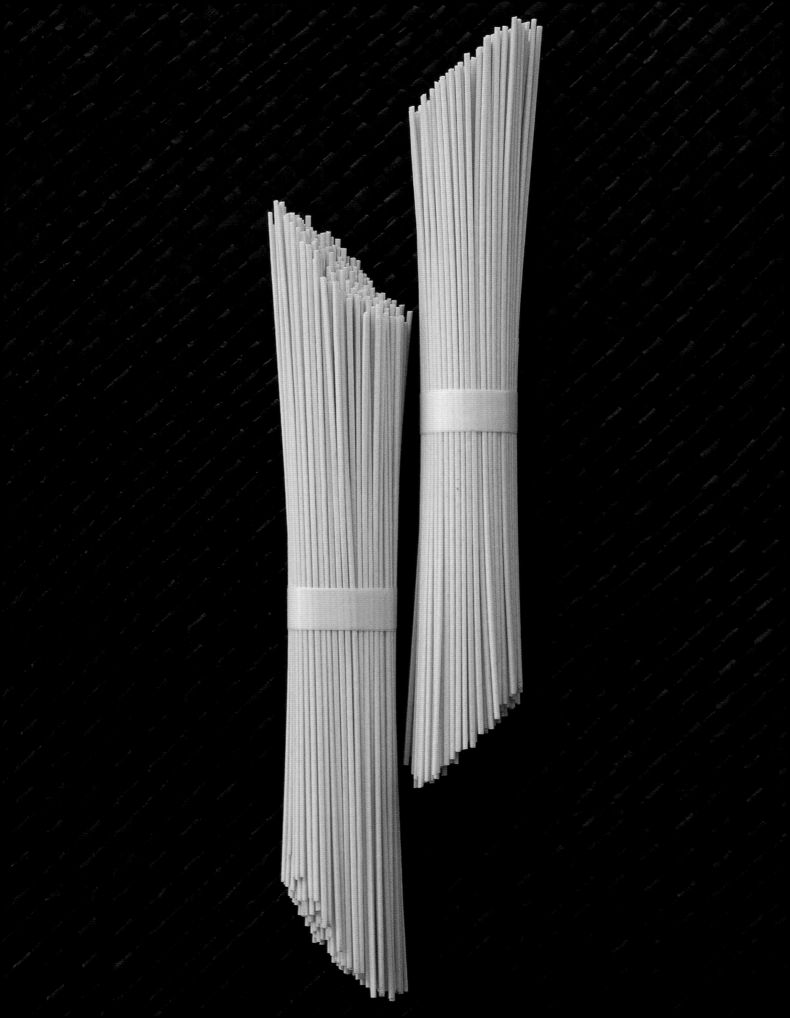

Noodle id 15 Ramen

What

Ramen are not really Japanese, but are based on the Chinese wheat noodle (the name simply means Chinese noodle), and are popular vending machine and supermarket snacks, sold as cup noodles or instant noodles. Japanese noodle purists refuse to recognise them, but there is a noble side to ramen. In Japan, they are also sold by street vendors late at night, and by specialist noodle houses who generally serve the noodles with hot broth, topped with fish cake and pork slices.

Why

For exactly the same reason that wheat noodles are so popular, not only all over Asia, but the world. They're no fuss, they're basic, they're recognisable, they're easy, and they make you feel good.

Where

Ramen are popular all over Japan. In western Japan they are more commonly known as chuka soba, which are pre-cooked, then dried.

Which

Ramen can be purchased in an instant form, either in a cup or a plastic pack, usually with a sachet of instant broth. They are also sold dried (shown). Normal Chinese dried egg noodles are a perfect substitute, but fresh, uncooked ramen are best if you're going to cook them in the traditional way in a broth. If you come across a pack in your Japanese supermarket labelled yakisoba, it does not contain soba but ramen intended for use in stir fries.

How

Fresh: Boil in plenty of salted water for about 2 minutes. Rinse in cold water, drain and set aside.

Dried: Cook in boiling water for 3 to 4 minutes. Rinse in cold water, drain and set aside.

Instant: Heat according to directions on the pack, although you wouldn't find a true noodle lover within 20 metres of an instant noodle.

Whatever

Ramen is the only noodle known to have starred in its own full-length 'noodle eastern' feature film, Juzo Itami's Tampopo. Get it on video, and learn the way of the noodle.

Recipes

Ramen with char sieu (page 107); Five mushroom miso with ramen (page 111).

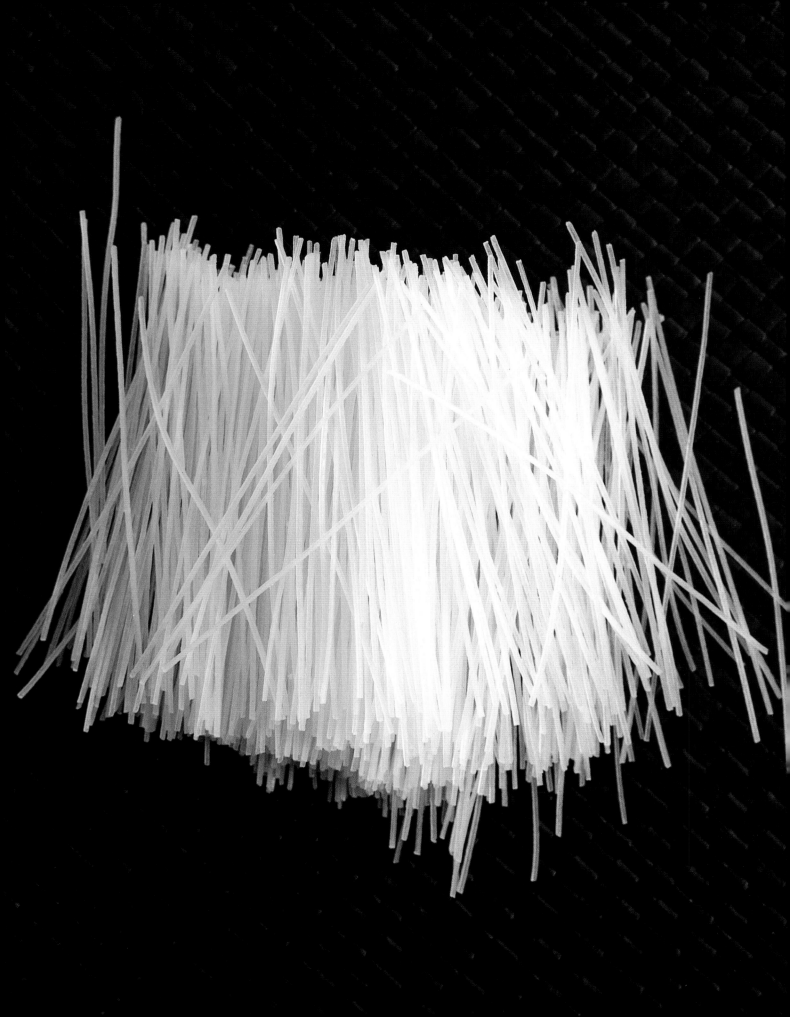

What
Thin, delicate noodles that resemble straight, thin bean thread noodles. They are usually made from potato and corn starches but are sometimes made from mung bean starch, when they are known as ryokuto harusame. They are usually white or pale cream, and semi-transparent in appearance, and are popular for use in one-pot dishes, soups and salads. They can also be used as a substitute for shirataki (see Noodle i-d 17) in sukiyaki. The name harusame actually means spring rain, suggested perhaps by the poetically light, translucent nature of these fine, pretty filaments.

Why
Because of their nicely chewy texture, quite gorgeous see-through appearance, and sheer versatility.

Where
While decidedly Japanese in nature, harusame are also popular in Korea, where they are combined mainly with shellfish, such as clams, prawns and crabs.

Which
Harusame are sold dried in little plastic packets, which generally hold around 100 g (3½ oz). They vary in length from 12 to 15 cm (5 to 6 in) and can be very fine and wire-like in appearance or flat and thin. Sometimes called salad noodles, they can be found in Japanese supermarkets or Korean food shops.

How
Before use, soak the noodles in hot water and let stand for about 5 minutes. Rinse under cold water and drain thoroughly. Set aside until needed.

Whatever
Like rice vermicelli, harusame respond quite dramatically when deep fried. For this reason, they are popular in Japan as a prickly, theatrical coating for deep-fried tempura.

Recipes
Spring rain tempura (page 92–3).

What

Not strictly noodles in the flour and water sense, shirataki are actually fine strands of konnyaku, a jelly-like paste made from the root *Amorphophallus konjac*, a Japanese yam known more commonly as devil's tongue plant. This explains shirataki's sinister nickname of 'devil's tongue noodles'. While there's no reason why they can't be added to braised dishes and soups, shirataki are most commonly associated with sukiyaki, a cook-at-the-table dish of beef and vegetables. The name shirataki actually means 'white waterfall' due to their shimmering appearance. That's worth creating a small haiku while cooking, surely.

Why

Texture, yet again. These 'noodles' are all about mouth feel. When combined with another ingredient, they seem to become a part of it, adding a lovely, slippery bounce to something else's flavour.

Where

Japan, but more specifically, the sukiyaki pots of Japan, although similar noodles also turn up in Korea.

Which

Usually shirataki come suspended in water in clear, sausage-shaped plastic packets, kept in the fridge at Japanese food stores. They are sometimes also available in cans, which isn't as much fun.

How

Drain the noodles after opening the 'sausage' and rinse well under cold water to remove the slightly artificial smell. They are now ready to use.

Whatever

While purists believe that sukiyaki isn't sukiyaki without shirataki, harusame or spring rain noodles (see Noodle i-d 16) can be substituted, as can normal bean thread vermicelli (see Noodle i-d 11), which are more readily available.

Recipes

Sukiyaki (page 102).

Noodle i-d **18** Naeng myun

What
The Korean answer to soba, naeng myun are chewier, and paler in appearance. These popular noodles are usually made from a combination of buckwheat flour and potato starch, although cornstarch is sometimes used. The name itself simply means 'cold noodle', which neatly sums up their most popular form of presentation. They are also served hot in soup.

Why
Because the flavour and the texture make them perfect for cold noodle soups, and because the hot Korean summers make it the perfect country for cold noodle soups.

Where
Naeng myun are very much a Korean phenomenon, although Japanese soba noodles can be substituted with great success.

Which
In Korean or Asian grocery stores, naeng myun can occasionally be found fresh/frozen, but the dried variety is easier to find (shown). Generally sold in 750 g (1½ lb) packs, they have a distinctive, almost plastic, sheen and a pale brown buckwheat colour.

How
Dried: Cook in boiling water for 3 to 4 minutes, or until cooked but still firm. Rinse in cold water, drain and set aside.
Fresh/frozen: Boil just long enough for them to thaw. Drain and chill.

Whatever
Once cooked, naeng myun can become unwieldy and awkward to handle. Therefore, a favourite trick of Korean cooks is to bring a pair of scissors to the dining table and to cut the noodles in every bowl into manageable lengths. Don't cut them too short, however, or you will spoil all the fun.

Recipes
Bibim naeng myun (page 160); Mul naeng myun (page 164).

What
A bigger, tougher, longer, stronger cousin of bean thread vermicelli (see Noodle i-d 11), these shimmering, translucent noodles are actually made from sweet potato starch. They require a fair amount of chewing and are popular in soups and stir-fries. While normal bean thread noodles can be substituted, they won't feel quite as substantial. Dang myun's major role is in one of Korea's most famous dishes, chap chae, a stir fry of noodles, beef and vegetables.

Why
The beauty of these otherwise drab-looking noodles lies in their resilient, chewy nature and ability to soak up flavours around them like gastronomic blotting paper.

Where
While transparent noodles are found all over Asia, dang myun is in a class of its own, and is very much a Korean phenomenon, highly sought after by the Korean noodle lover.

Which
These distinctive noodles are greyish in colour and are sold dried in 30 cm (12 in) lengths.

How
Soak in hot water for about 10 to 15 minutes to soften, then rinse in cold water and drain well. Alternatively, cook in plenty of boiling water for about 3 minutes until they are cooked, but not sloppy. Rinse well in cold water, and drain thoroughly. Set aside until needed.

Whatever
Unfortunately, most dang myun noodles imported from Korea, including the popular Assi brand, aren't actually labelled dang myun on the pack because the manufacturers think we wouldn't know what we were looking for. So look for the words 'Korean vermicelli' and check the list of ingredients for 'sweet potato starch'. Only then can you be sure.

Recipes
Chap chae (page 158–9); Mandu kuk (page 162);
Mu chungol (page 163).

Noodle i-d 20 Gooksu

What

Gooksu is the generic term for noodle in Korean, although the word usually refers to these long wheat flour noodles. Gooksu, or Korean 'knife cut' noodles, were traditionally made at home with wheat flour, egg and water, and cut into long, thin, pale strips. These days, however, they're more likely to be bought dried, from Korean and Asian food stores. They are generally served in soups, and accompanied by spicy kim chee, fermented cabbage. Their most famous incarnation is kalgooksu, a spicy, anchovy-flavoured soup.

Why

Because it's an earthy, satisfying sort of noodle, one that deserves a good slurp, and good friends to share it with. Or because you're Korean.

Where

Although they bear more than a passing resemblance to udon noodles (but neater and thinner), these noodles are very much a Korean specialty, and star attractions of the many noodle shops that make Seoul such a satisfying noodle city.

Which

Dried gooksu noodles are usually sold in 1 kg (2 lb) packs. They are straight, white and come in both round and flat versions. The round ones are usually used in soups, while the flat are preferred for stir-fried dishes.

How

Cook dried noodles in plenty of water at a rolling boil for 3 to 4 minutes. The noodles need to remain al dente, so be careful not to overcook. Rinse under cold water and drain thoroughly. Set aside until needed.

Whatever

One former Korean prime minister loved these noodles so much that, instead of holding state banquets for visiting diplomats, he would take them home to sample his wife's famous kalgooksu.

Recipes

Kalgooksu (page 161).

China

China-Beijing
Brown sauce noodles
(Zha jiang mian) 48
Eggflower noodle soup 50
China-Chiu Chow
Chiu Chow dessert noodles 51
China-Guangdong
Hor fun soup noodles with roast duck 52
Beef and water spinach noodles 54
Chicken chow mein 55
Chicken noodle soup 56
Fried hor fun with beef 57
Long-life noodles 58
Roast pork noodle soup 59
Wonton soup with noodles 60
Two-sides-brown noodles with
shredded duck 62
Buddhist vegetable noodles 63
China-Far North
Noodles with shredded lamb 64
China-Shanghai
Lion's head meatballs 66
Hokkien noodles with prawns 67
Shanghai pork noodles 68

Stir-fried Shanghai noodles 70

China-Sichuan

Ants climbing trees 71

Cold noodles with spicy
Sichuan sauce 72

Dan dan mian 73

Sichuan noodle-shop noodles 74

Sichuan beef noodle soup 75

Sichuan fish noodles 76

China-Yunan

Cross the bridge noodles 78

China-Modern

Bang bang chicken noodles 79

Chicken noodle salad 80

Dry-cooked green beans
with noodles 81

Gung Bao chicken with
Shanghai noodles 82

Noodles with pork and pickles 83

Eight treasure noodles 84

San choy bau with cellophane
noodles 86

Suckling pig, jellyfish and
noodle salad 87

Brown sauce noodles (Zha jiang mian)

As if there weren't enough arguments over whether it was the Italians or the Chinese who invented noodles (they both did), we are now getting into who invented the Bolognese sauce as well. Here, it is brown bean instead of tomato and pork instead of veal, but we can still feel gratitude for having both in the world.

4 tbsp brown bean sauce
1 tbsp hoisin sauce
½ cup chicken stock
½ tsp sugar
2 tbsp peanut or corn oil
5 spring onions, white part, chopped
1 tbsp finely chopped garlic
500 g (1 lb) minced pork
400 g (14 oz) fresh Shanghai noodles
1 cucumber, cut into long matchsticks
2 spring onions, green part, finely sliced
1 cup bean sprouts, blanched

Mash brown bean sauce with the back of a spoon and mix well with hoisin sauce, stock and sugar.

Heat oil in a hot wok and fry the spring onion and garlic for 20 seconds. Add pork and stir fry until it separates into small pieces and is coloured, about 2 to 3 minutes. Add the bean mixture, reduce heat and simmer for 5 minutes.

Cook noodles in boiling water for 4 to 5 minutes. Drain and place in a large bowl. Spoon the brown sauce over them, and arrange a sheaf of cucumber strips on top. Serve with more cucumber strips, spring onion greens and bean sprouts, so that everyone can help themselves, folding the goodies through the sauce and the noodles.

Serves four.

Eggflower noodle soup

This is a serious version of good old chicken and sweet corn soup, but without the chicken and the sweet corn. Poetic cooks insist the threads of egg look like chrysanthemum petals, but it is perfectly all right if they just look like threads of egg.

300 g (10 oz) pork belly
¼ cup dried wood fungus
8 dried shiitake mushrooms
2 tbsp peanut oil
1 tbsp minced fresh ginger
½ cup bamboo shoots, cut into matchsticks
4 cups chicken stock
1 tsp salt
2 tbsp soy sauce
1 tbsp shaohsing rice wine or dry sherry
350 g (11 oz) fresh flat egg noodles
½ cup ham, sliced into thin strips
1 tbsp cornflour, mixed with 1 tbsp water
2 eggs, beaten
1 tsp sesame oil
½ tsp pepper
3 spring onions, green part only, finely sliced

Put pork belly in a saucepan, cover with cold water and bring to the boil. Skim off any nasty stuff, reduce heat and simmer for 45 minutes. Turn off the heat and leave pork in the liquid to cool.

Soak the wood fungus and mushrooms separately in hot water for about an hour. Drain and rinse well, then cut into thin strips, discarding any stems.

Cut the cooled pork into thin strips about 3 cm (1 in) wide (reserve the cooking liquid, skimming off the fat).

Heat peanut oil in a saucepan and cook ginger, mushrooms, wood fungus and bamboo shoots and stir fry briefly. Add chicken stock and 4 cups of the pork cooking liquid and bring to the boil. Add salt, soy sauce and rice wine, taste, adjust seasonings, and simmer for 3 minutes.

Cook noodles in boiling water for about 1 minute. Drain, rinse in cold water and drain again. Return to the saucepan, off the heat, and keep warm.

Add pork and ham to the soup, turn up the heat and stir in the cornflour mixture. Stir until the soup thickens, lower heat and slowly pour the egg into the soup in a thin stream through the tines of a fork. Stir lightly, then add sesame oil and pepper. Divide noodles between 4 bowls. Ladle soup over and scatter with spring onions.

Serves four.

Chiu Chow dessert noodles

The Chiu Chow people live near the coast in the Province of Guangdong. While their food shares many of the subtleties of the Cantonese, flavours are often punched up with sharp, vinegary dipping sauces. Even their famous dessert noodles are given a good, solid kick along with the addition of a little red vinegar. This wonderfully simple dish is sweet and sour in its most sublime form.

100 g (3 oz) dried egg noodles
2 tbsp peanut oil
3 tbsp Chinese red vinegar
3 tbsp white sugar

Put noodles in a pot of boiling water and simmer for 3 minutes, or until tender. Rinse under cold, running water and drain thoroughly. Set aside for 2 hours, then pat dry.

Heat oil in a hot wok and swirl around to cover the surface. Put noodles in the wok and flatten them against the surface, pressing them with the back of a ladle. Cook for about 5 minutes, until golden and crisp on the underside. Place a large plate on top of the wok and invert the wok so that the flat noodle pancake tips out onto the plate. Slide the pancake back in and cook on the other side.

Cut pancake into 4. Serve with side bowls of red vinegar and white sugar. Sprinkle both on top, to your own taste, and eat with chopsticks or fork and spoon.

Serves four.

Hor fun soup noodles with roast duck

How easy is this? All it takes is some rice noodles, a ladleful of chicken stock and couple of pieces of the Cantonese roast duck you picked up at the Chinese barbecued meats shop on the way home. It goes to show that there are times when shopping skills are more important than cooking skills.

2 cloves of garlic, crushed with the side of a knife blade
2 slices ginger, cut into thin matchsticks
1 tbsp oyster sauce
2 litres (3½ pts) chicken stock
4 iceberg lettuce leaves
½ Cantonese roast duck (from Chinese barbecued meats shop)
300 g (10 oz) fresh rice sheet noodles
2 spring onions, green part only, sliced

Add garlic, ginger and oyster sauce to chicken stock and simmer for 5 minutes. Remove garlic. Blanch lettuce leaves quickly in the stock and remove. Chop duck Chinese-style, through the bone, into 2.5 cm (1 in) pieces.

Cut rice sheet noodles into strips about 2 cm (¾ in) wide and place in a bowl. Pour boiling water over the top, and quickly but carefully separate the noodles with a pair of chopsticks. Drain and divide among 4 soup bowls. Arrange lettuce leaf on top, and ladle hot soup over the noodles. Put 4 or 5 pieces of duck in each bowl and sprinkle with spring onion.

Serves four.

China – Guangdong   *Noodle i-d* **7**

Beef and water spinach noodles

Water spinach, known as *ong choy* in Cantonese, is a seductive, velvety vegetable that adds a little touch of luxury to anything it comes near. From the subtle crunch of its hollow stems to the intense sweetness of its leaves, it is one of the least boring green vegetables you'll ever meet. Here it turns a homely bowl of beef noodles into something with real depth and character.

200 g (7 oz) beef (scotch fillet or rump)
1 tbsp cornflour
3 tbsp soy sauce
1 tsp sugar
1 tsp shaohsing rice wine, or dry sherry
4 tbsp peanut oil
300 g (10 oz) dried wheat noodles
400 g (14 oz) water spinach (*ong choy*), thoroughly washed
2 spring onions, finely sliced
1 tbsp ginger, grated
2 cloves of garlic, finely chopped
1 tbsp hoisin sauce
2 tbsp chicken stock
½ tsp salt
pinch of black pepper

Finely slice meat into thin strips 5 cm (2 in) long. Rub cornflour into the meat, combine with 1 tablespoon soy sauce, the sugar, rice wine and 1 tablespoon oil, and leave to marinate for an hour.

Cook noodles in plenty of salted, boiling water for about 4 minutes, or until tender, then rinse well under cold water, drain and set aside.

Cut water spinach into 6 in (2½ in) pieces.

Heat 2 tablespoons oil in a hot wok and stir fry water spinach for a minute or two, moving continuously. Remove spinach, set aside and add 1 more tablespoon of oil to the wok. Stir fry beef for 1 minute, add half the spring onion, the ginger, garlic and hoisin sauce and stir fry for another minute over high heat. Add remaining 2 tablespoons soy sauce, stock, salt and black pepper. When the liquid starts to boil, add the noodles and water spinach and heat through, stirring well to combine. Sprinkle with spring onion and serve.

Serves four.

Chicken chow mein

Better known as number 42 (or 17, or 91), this would have to be the world's most boring, safe, unadventurous, and uneventful Chinese order ever. Yet somewhere beyond the gluggy cornflour sauce, the tired, limp vegetables and that back-of-the-tongue thwack of MSG is something pure, noble, and down-right nice that deserves reclaiming.

300 g (10 oz) dried egg noodles
200 g (7 oz) boned chicken meat
150 g (5 oz) pork loin
2 tbsp soy sauce
2 tsp grated ginger
1 tbsp shaohsing rice wine, or dry sherry
1½ tbsp cornflour
6 dried mushrooms, soaked in hot water for 1 hour
6 stems choy sum (flowering cabbage)
3 tbsp peanut oil
4 spring onions, cut into 2.5 cm (1 in) lengths
2 tsp sesame oil
½ cup chicken stock
2 extra spring onions, green part only, finely sliced

Cook noodles in boiling salted water for 3 to 4 minutes, or until tender. Drain, rinse in cold water, drain again, cover and set aside.

Cut chicken and pork into thin strips. Combine 1 tablespoon soy sauce with ginger, rice wine and 1 tablespoon cornflour. Add meat and marinate for 30 minutes.

Cut stems off mushrooms and slice caps into thin strips. Wash choy sum and cut into 5 cm (2 in) pieces. Put thicker stems in boiling water and cook for a minute. Add thinner stems and leaves and cook for a further 30 seconds. Drain and refresh with cold water.

Heat 2 tablespoons peanut oil in a hot wok and stir fry the meats for 1 minute. Add choy sum, mushroom and spring onion and cook for 2 minutes. Remove from the wok. Add 1 more tablespoon oil to hot wok and stir fry noodles for about 3 minutes. Return meat and vegetables to wok, along with the sesame oil and remaining 1 tablespoon soy sauce. Toss well. Add chicken stock and remaining cornflour, mixed to a paste with a little water (use less cornflour if the mixture is already starting to thicken). Transfer to a large serving plate and sprinkle with spring onion.

Serves four.

Chicken noodle soup

Forget your packets, cans, pretend noodles and powdered, super-boosted chicken essences. Real chicken noodle soup is made from real chicken stock, with real chicken pieces and the freshest egg noodles you can lay your hands on. They usually come in a large plastic packet and that's the only packet you'll ever really need for chicken noodle soup.

1 tsp salt
1 egg white, lightly beaten
2 tsp cornflour
2 chicken breasts, cut into thin strips
8 dried shiitake mushrooms, soaked
350 g (11 oz) fresh flat egg noodles
1 tbsp peanut oil
100 g (3 oz) bamboo shoots, cut into thin matchsticks
½ bunch choy sum (flowering cabbage) leaves, about 200 g (7 oz), roughly chopped
3 spring onions, cut into 2.5 cm (1 in) lengths
2 tbsp light soy sauce
1 tbsp shaohsing rice wine, or dry sherry
1 tsp sugar
1 tsp sesame oil
2 litres (3½ pts) chicken stock, simmering

Combine ½ teaspoon of salt, egg white and cornflour in a bowl, add chicken and toss to coat. Leave for 20 minutes to 'velvet' the chicken. Drain mushrooms, remove stems and slice caps finely.

Cook noodles in boiling water for 2 minutes, rinse in cold water and drain well.

Heat oil in a hot wok and stir fry chicken, bamboo shoots and mushrooms for 2 minutes. Add choy sum and spring onion and stir fry for another minute. Add soy sauce, rice wine, sugar, sesame oil and ½ teaspoon salt.

Add noodles to the stock and return to the boil. Add the contents of the wok, stir through and serve in Chinese bowls with soup spoons and chopsticks.

Serves four.

Fried hor fun with beef

The Cantonese consider the feel or texture of food to be just as important, if not more important, than the flavour. Here, the overriding quality is slipperiness. The beef is marinated with cornflour to give it a smooth, silky feel, while the already slinky rice noodles are made even slinkier by mixing them with the 'cooked-oil' sauce. The end result feels like a delicious, edible slippery dip.

500 g (1 lb) fresh rice sheet noodles
1 tsp peanut oil, for noodles
4 tbsp peanut oil
200 g (7 oz) lean beef, thinly sliced
1 tsp light soy sauce
1 tsp cornflour, mixed with 1 tbsp cold water
1 tsp sugar
2 tbsp dark soy sauce
2 tbsp light soy sauce
2 slices of ginger, cut into fine matchsticks
2 spring onions, finely chopped
1 cup bean sprouts, rinsed

Cut rice sheets into 2 cm (¾ in) strips, if not already cut. Place in a heatproof bowl and pour boiling water over to cover, gently shake strips apart with a pair of chopsticks. Drain and cool under cold running water. Drain well and mix with 1 teaspoon peanut oil to prevent sticking.

Heat 4 tablespoons peanut oil in a hot wok, cook for 2 minutes, then cool. Mix 2 tablespoons of this cooked oil with beef, 1 teaspoon light soy sauce and cornflour mixture, and marinate for 30 minutes. Mix sugar, dark and light soy sauces and set aside.

Heat remaining 2 tablespoons cooked oil in a hot wok and cook ginger and spring onion for 1 minute before removing. Add beef mixture and stir fry for 1 minute until it changes colour. Add bean sprouts to wok and fry for 1 minute. Lift out and set aside. Add drained noodles and stir fry for 2 minutes. Add combined sugar and soy sauces and stir well. Return beef to the wok and stir, mixing thoroughly. Serve on a large platter or in small Chinese bowls.

Serves four.

China—Guangdong   *Noodle i-d 7*

Long-life noodles

No celebration or banquet is complete without a dish of long-life noodles, served either at the beginning or the very end. The idea is simple: the longer the noodle, the longer you will live. And of course, the longer you live, the more long-life noodles you will get to eat. There is something rather endearing about Chinese logic.

4 spring onions
8 dried shiitake mushrooms, soaked
1 large e-fu noodle cake, about 350 g (11 oz)
2 tbsp soy sauce
1 tbsp oyster sauce
1 tsp sesame oil
1 tsp sugar
¾ cup chicken stock
1 tbsp peanut oil
1 tbsp grated ginger
2 cloves of garlic, crushed with the side of a knife blade

Finely slice the green tops of the spring onions and reserve. Cut the remainder into matchsticks. Drain mushrooms, discard stems and slice caps finely.

Cook noodles in boiling water for 3 to 4 minutes. Rinse in cold water and drain well.

Mix soy sauce, oyster sauce, sesame oil, sugar and chicken stock in a bowl and set aside.

Heat peanut oil in a hot wok and stir fry ginger and garlic for 1 minute. Add spring onion matchsticks, all of the mushrooms and sauce ingredients and bring to the boil, stirring. Cook for 1 minute. Add noodles and cook for about 2 minutes, or until they have absorbed most of the sauce. Serve immediately, scattered with the spring onion greens.

Serves four.

Roast pork noodle soup

No self-respecting noodle lover should ever live more than a short drive from a Chinese barbecued meats shop. Of course, you can make your own char sieu (see Basics, page 189) and keep it in the fridge, but that way, you can't pick up a piece of suckling pig and a little white cut chicken at the same time.

200 g (7 oz) dried wheat noodles
½ bunch gai laan (Chinese broccoli), about 350 g (11 oz)
3 tbsp peanut oil
6 slices of ginger, cut into matchsticks
1 tbsp shaohsing rice wine, or dry sherry
2 tbsp oyster sauce
2 tbsp soy sauce
½ tsp salt
pinch of black pepper
2 tsp sugar
½ tsp sesame oil
1 tbsp cornflour, mixed with a little water
200 g (7 oz) char sieu (red roast pork), cut into thin slices
2 spring onions, sliced on the diagonal into 2.5 cm (1 in) lengths
2 litres (3½ pts) chicken stock
1 spring onion, green part only, sliced into 2.5 cm (1 in) lengths

Cook noodles in plenty of salted, boiling water for 4 minutes, or until tender, then rinse well under cold water, drain and set aside.

Cut gai laan into 6 cm (2½ in) pieces. Put thick stems in a pot of boiling water and cook for 1 minute. Add leaves and thinner stems and cook for 20 seconds. Remove from pot and plunge into cold water. When cool, drain and set aside.

Heat peanut oil in a hot wok and stir fry ginger for 1 minute, add gai laan and stir fry for another minute. Add rice wine, oyster sauce, soy sauce, salt, pepper, sugar, sesame oil and cornflour mixture. When liquid starts to boil, add pork and spring onion and heat through, stirring.

In a separate pot, bring chicken stock to the boil. Put noodles in a strainer or colander and pour boiling water over the top to warm them. Drain well. To serve, put a handful of noodles into each of 4 bowls. Pour chicken stock over noodles and top with pork mixture. Scatter spring onion on top and serve with spoons and chopsticks.

Serves four.

China–Guangdong   *Noodle i-d 1*   59

Wonton soup with noodles

If there were one dish that summed up everything that was good, pure and nourishing about Cantonese food, this would be it. It is subtle, gentle, fragrant, thoroughly clean tasting and almost a monument to the freshness and quality of the ingredients that go into its making. The Chinese eat it for a full-on breakfast, a fast lunch, a satisfying supper and, sometimes, for a homely, easy dinner. In other words, all the time.

150 g (5 oz) raw prawns, peeled, deveined and finely minced
150 g (5 oz) minced pork
2 tbsp pork or bacon fat, finely minced
4 dried shiitake mushrooms, soaked and finely minced
4 water chestnuts, finely chopped
2 spring onions, white part only, finely chopped
1 small egg white
salt and pepper
200 g (7 oz) fresh egg noodles
1 packet fresh wonton wrappers
1 heaped tsp cornflour mixed with 1 tbsp cold water
2 litres (3½ pts) chicken stock
2 slices ginger, peeled
100 g (3 oz) choy sum (flowering cabbage), washed and roughly sliced
2 spring onions, green part only, sliced

To make dumpling mixture, combine prawn, pork, pork fat, mushroom, water chestnuts, spring onion, egg white, salt and pepper in a bowl and mix with your hands until totally amalgamated. Refrigerate for 1 hour.

Cook noodles in boiling water for 1 to 2 minutes. Drain, rinse with cold water, drain again and set aside.

Lay a wonton skin on the workbench. Put a teaspoon of filling in the centre. Dip your finger in the cornflour paste and run it around the edges. Fold over to form a triangle, pressing the edges together. Bring the 2 extreme corners together to meet and overlap in the middle, and seal with a little paste. Make 4 or 5 dumplings per person.

Heat stock in a saucepan, add ginger and bring to a simmer. Blanch cabbage in boiling water for 1 minute, drain and add to stock. Drop dumplings in a pot of boiling water and cook until they float to the surface, about 2 minutes. Drain and distribute among 4 deep warmed soup bowls. Pour boiling water over noodles in a strainer over the sink to warm. Drain and divide among the bowls. Discard ginger and pour stock on top. Scatter with spring onion.

Serves four.

China—Guangdong   *Noodle i-d 2*   61

Two-sides-brown noodles with shredded duck

It may seem something of a pointless exercise, creating a crisp, crunchy noodle pancake just so you can pour sauce all over it, and make the noodles go soggy again. But that is exactly the point. If you don't get it now, you will with your first mouthful.

200 g (7 oz) dried wheat noodles (thin)
4 tbsp peanut oil
2 cloves of garlic, crushed with the side of a knife blade
2 slices fresh ginger
1 bunch choy sum (flowering cabbage), cut into 5 cm (2 in) sections
6 shiitake mushrooms, soaked for 1 hour, and sliced
100 g (3 oz) bamboo shoots, cut into matchsticks
8 water chestnuts, sliced thinly
1 lup cheong sausage, cut into matchsticks
meat from ½ Chinese roast duck, sliced finely
1 cup bean sprouts, rinsed
1 tbsp oyster sauce
1 tbsp soy sauce
½ cup chicken stock
1 tsp cornflour
1 tbsp shaohsing rice wine, or dry sherry
3 spring onions, finely sliced

Drop noodles into a pot of boiling water and cook for about 4 minutes. Rinse under cold water and drain well.

Heat 2 tablespoons peanut oil in a hot wok and cook 1 clove of garlic and 1 slice of ginger for a minute to flavour the oil, then remove. Add thicker choy sum stems and stir fry for 2 minutes. Add mushroom, bamboo shoot, water chestnuts, lup cheong and duck and stir fry for 2 minutes. Add choy sum leaves and bean sprouts and stir fry until they soften. Add oyster sauce, soy sauce and stock and toss lightly. Mix cornflour with rice wine and stir into the mixture. Tip everything into a heatproof bowl and keep warm in a low oven.

Heat remaining peanut oil in a hot wok and cook remaining ginger and garlic for 1 minute until golden, then discard. Tip noodles into wok and flatten them against the surface. Cook for 4 to 5 minutes until golden brown. Place a flat plate on top of the wok and invert the whole thing so that the noodle pancake falls onto the plate. Return wok to heat, add a little extra oil, slide pancake back in and cook the other side. Turn out on a large, warmed serving platter and top with stir-fried mixture and spring onion.

Serves four.

Buddhist vegetable noodles

In China, Buddhist monks go to extreme lengths to create vegetarian food that looks, smells and even tastes like fish or meat. For me, however, the most successful vegetable dishes in the Chinese repertoire are those that look like vegetables. This recipe is based on a classic Buddhist vegetarian dish that manages to satisfy both aesthetically and gastronomically.

3 tbsp peanut oil
1 small onion, sliced lengthwise
2 slices ginger, finely chopped
8 dried shiitake mushrooms, soaked and sliced (reserve soaking water)
2 cloves of garlic, finely chopped
1 tbsp vegetarian oyster sauce (yes, it does exist, see Glossary, page 196)
3 tbsp light soy sauce
½ red capsicum, thinly sliced
½ green capsicum, thinly sliced
½ medium carrot, thinly sliced
3 tbsp bamboo shoots, cut into matchsticks
2 cups shredded Tientsin cabbage
1 cup bean sprouts, rinsed
½ tsp salt
pinch of white pepper
½ tsp sugar
2 tsp sesame oil
1 tbsp shaohsing rice wine, or dry sherry
300 g (10 oz) fresh egg noodles
1 tsp peanut oil
2 spring onions, green part only, finely sliced

Heat 1 tablespoon oil in a hot wok and stir fry onion until translucent. Add ginger, mushrooms and garlic and cook for another minute. Add oyster sauce and 2 tablespoons soy sauce and cook for another 30 seconds. Transfer wok contents to a bowl. Heat 2 tablespoons oil in the wok and stir fry capsicum, carrot, bamboo shoots and cabbage for 3 minutes on high heat. Add bean sprouts, salt, pepper, sugar and 4 tablespoons reserved mushroom water, and cook for 1 minute. Add onion and mushroom mixture, sesame oil and rice wine and combine well.

Cook noodles in plenty of water at a rolling boil for about 1 minute. Drain thoroughly, rinse under cold running water, and drain well. Toss with remaining 1 tablespoon soy sauce and 1 teaspoon oil. Put noodles on a large warmed serving platter, spoon on vegetable mixture and mix lightly. Sprinkle with spring onion and serve.

Serves four.

Noodles with shredded lamb

In the south of China, lamb is very rare, and the Cantonese, not great fans of its smell or taste, are easily able to distinguish 'mutton-eaters' by their smell. But up north, lamb means survival, and the meat features in countless regional specialties. This simple dish combines lamb and noodles in an easy, ingenious way that even a Cantonese could learn to love.

200 g (7 oz) bean thread vermicelli
200 g (7 oz) lamb fillet
1 egg, beaten
1 tbsp cornflour
½ tsp salt
2 tbsp water
2 tbsp peanut oil
3 tbsp soy sauce
3 spring onions, green part only, cut into 5 cm (2 in) lengths
1 cup chicken stock
1 tsp sesame oil
2 tbsp shaohsing rice wine, or dry sherry

Put noodles in a bowl, pour boiling water over them and leave to stand for 3 to 4 minutes. Rinse in cold water, drain and set aside.

Cut lamb into thin strips. Combine the beaten egg, cornflour, salt and water in a bowl. Add lamb and coat well with the mixture and set aside for 10 to 15 minutes.

Heat peanut oil in a hot wok and stir fry lamb for 1 or 2 minutes. Add soy sauce and spring onion and stir fry for another minute. Add chicken stock, noodles, sesame oil and rice wine and cook for a further 2 minutes. Serve on a large warmed platter or in Chinese bowls.

Serves four.

Lion's head meatballs

The extremely romantic name suggests that these giant, moist meatballs, when surrounded by a 'mane' of cabbage and noodles, look just like lions' heads. Yeah, right. The soft, light, almost moussey meatballs are traditionally made by repeatedly bashing the meat against the side of the bowl to break down its structure, but you can whiz it in the food processor instead for a similar result. A hint: for Chinese cooking, minced pork from an Asian butcher is always preferable to that from a non-Asian butcher.

6 dried Chinese mushrooms
100 g (3 oz) bean thread vermicelli
600 g (19 oz) minced pork
1 egg white
3 spring onions, chopped
2 slices ginger, finely chopped
1 tbsp cornflour
1 tbsp shaohsing rice wine, or dry sherry
salt, to taste
2 tbsp peanut oil
2 tbsp soy sauce
3 cups chicken stock, heated
4 small bak choy (cabbage)

Pour boiling water over mushrooms and leave to stand for about an hour. When soaked, lightly squeeze dry and discard the stems. Pour boiling water over the noodles and leave for 3 to 4 minutes to soften. Rinse in cold water, drain and set aside until needed.

Put pork, egg white, spring onion, ginger, cornflour, rice wine and salt in a food processor and blend until smooth. With your hands, shape the mixture into large meatballs about 5 cm (2 in) in diameter. Roll meatballs in a little extra cornflour. Heat oil and fry meatballs until lightly golden.

Add mushrooms, soy sauce and chicken stock to meatballs in a clay pot or flameproof casserole with a lid and bring to the boil. Cover, reduce heat and cook gently for 45 minutes.

Clean bak choy, cut in half lengthwise and add with noodles to the clay pot. Cook for a further 10 minutes. Bring the pot to the table to serve.

Serves four.

Hokkien noodles with prawns

Please try to put any passing resemblance between this and combination chow mein out of your mind. This is an intriguing, 'soft' combination of flavour and texture, lit up by the surprising, gentle Shanghainese sweetness that comes from the sugar and the ketchup.

500 g (1 lb) Hokkien noodles
200 g (7 oz) small raw prawns, peeled
½ tsp salt
3 tsp cornflour
200 g (7 oz) pork loin
3 tbsp soy sauce
4 tbsp peanut oil
2 small onions (or 4 shallots), finely sliced
¾ cup chicken stock
1 tbsp tomato sauce (ketchup)
1 tbsp sugar
1 tsp sesame oil

Put noodles in a heatproof bowl, cover with boiling water and leave for 1 minute. Drain well and set aside. Mix prawns with a pinch of salt and 1 teaspoon cornflour. Cut pork into thin strips and mix with 1 tablespoon soy sauce and 1 teaspoon cornflour and leave to stand for 20 minutes.

Heat 2 tablespoons oil in a hot wok and stir fry prawns quickly for 1 minute. Remove from wok. Add another tablespoon of oil and stir fry pork for about 2 minutes. Remove from wok. Add 1 tablespoon of oil and cook onion until soft. Add 2 tablespoons soy sauce, the stock, salt to taste, tomato ketchup, sugar and sesame oil.

Bring to the boil, add noodles and cook for 1 to 2 minutes. Return pork and prawns to the hot wok and toss well. Mix remaining teaspoon of cornflour with a teaspoon of water and stir through until the sauce thickens slightly. Serve on a warm platter or in small Chinese bowls.

Serves four.

Shanghai pork noodles

I tried to make this dish more difficult. I tried to make the recipe longer. I tried to make it complicated and confusing. But no matter what I did, it still worked out to be one of the simplest, fastest and most foolproof dishes in the whole book. Essentially, it's a Cantonese stir fry, with a bit of added interest.

4 dried shiitake mushrooms
2 tbsp dried shrimp
300 g (10 oz) rice vermicelli
75 g (2½ oz) pork loin
1 baby leek
2 tbsp peanut oil
1 stalk of celery, finely chopped
50 g (2 oz) bamboo shoots, cut into matchsticks
1 tsp salt
1 tsp sugar
½ cup chicken stock
2 tbsp soy sauce

Soak mushrooms in warm water for 1 hour, then drain. Cut off and discard stems and slice caps finely. Soak dried shrimp in warm water for 30 minutes, then drain. Pour boiling water over noodles and leave to soak for 6 to 7 minutes until tender. Drain and set aside until needed. Cut pork and leek into matchstick strips.

Heat oil in a hot wok and stir fry pork for 1 minute. Add shrimp, celery, bamboo shoots and leek, and stir fry for 1 minute. Add noodles and toss through. Add salt, sugar, stock and soy sauce, and cook until liquid has been absorbed by the noodles.

Serves four.

Stir-fried Shanghai noodles

A simple stir fry technique produces a surprisingly complex, and many-layered dish, underlaid by the gorgeously silky quality of the Shanghai noodles. You can use any kind of Chinese cabbage, but the even, uniform crunch of the white Tientsin, or Peking cabbage, makes it a natural.

400 g (14 oz) Shanghai noodles
1 tsp sesame oil
100 g (3 oz) lean pork
100 g (3 oz) chicken thigh meat
3 tbsp peanut oil
350 g (11 oz) Tientsin cabbage, finely shredded
1 stalk of celery, cut into small dice
1 cup chicken stock
¼ tsp white pepper
3 tbsp dark soy sauce

Boil noodles in plenty of simmering water for 4 to 5 minutes. Drain, rinse in cold water and drain again. Toss with sesame oil and set aside until needed.

Cut pork and chicken into thin strips. Heat peanut oil in a hot wok and stir fry meats for 1 minute. Add cabbage and celery and stir fry for 2 minutes. Add noodles and stir fry for a further minute. Add stock, white pepper and dark soy sauce and stir fry until liquid has been absorbed by the noodles. Serve on a warm platter or in small Chinese bowls.

Serves four.

Ants climbing trees

A Chinese chef once told me that when a Chinese diner drops a glass at a banquet, that person would never say, 'Oops, I dropped a glass.' Instead, they would say, 'It falls like an opening blossom, rich and noble.' The Sichuanese have an equally poetic way with food. This dish can actually look like ants climbing trees, especially if you drink enough *mui kwe lu* rose wine.

250 g (8 oz) minced pork
2 tbsp light soy sauce
1 tbsp sugar
1 tsp cornflour
1 tbsp chilli bean paste
200 g (7 oz) bean thread vermicelli
3 tbsp peanut oil
1 spring onion, finely chopped
1 small red chilli, finely chopped
½ cup chicken stock
1 tbsp dark soy sauce
1 spring onion, green part only, thinly sliced

Combine pork, light soy sauce, sugar, cornflour and chilli bean paste and leave to stand for 20 minutes.

Pour boiling water over noodles in a heatproof bowl and let stand for 3 to 4 minutes until tender. Drain.

Heat oil in a hot wok and cook chopped spring onion and chilli for about 30 seconds. Add pork mixture and stir fry for 2 to 3 minutes, then add noodles and mix well.

Add chicken stock and dark soy sauce and bring to the boil. Cook for a few more minutes until the liquid has all but disappeared into the noodles. Scatter with sliced spring onion and serve.

Serves four.

Cold noodles with spicy Sichuan sauce

Beware, these cold noodles are hot, if you get my drift. Underscored by the prickly spice of Sichuan pepper, the fire of chilli bean sauce and the salty tickle of Sichuan pickle, this is pure Sichuan pleasure in a bowl.

1 chicken, about 1.2 kg (2½ lb), cooked
400 g (14 oz) fresh egg noodles
2 tsp sesame oil
3 tbsp peanut oil
2 tbsp light soy sauce
1 tbsp Sichuan chilli bean sauce
1 spring onion, finely sliced
1 tsp sugar
½ tsp salt
2 tbsp minced Sichuan preserved vegetable
1 tbsp roasted sesame seeds
½ cucumber, cut into fine matchsticks

Remove meat from chicken and shred into strips.

Put noodles in a pot of boiling water and cook for 1 to 2 minutes. Drain, rinse in cold water. Drain again, being careful to shake off all excess water. Toss noodles in sesame oil to prevent them from sticking and set aside to cool.

Heat peanut oil in a small pot until it is almost smoking. Remove from heat and add soy sauce, chilli bean sauce, spring onion, sugar, salt and preserved vegetable, stirring well. Leave to cool for about 20 minutes. Combine sauce with noodles, sesame seeds, cucumber and chicken.

Serves four.

Dan dan mian

The name of this dish translates as 'pole carrying noodles', referring to the shoulder poles that noodle sellers use to carry their edible wares. These days, the good people of Sichuan are more likely to eat this distinctively different, sweet, spicy, nutty dish in specialist dan dan noodle shops. It's hard to say who is going to like this dish more: noodle freaks or peanut butter addicts.

1 tsp peanut oil
1 tbsp ginger, grated
2 tsp sugar
1 cup bean sprouts
1 tbsp sesame seeds
2 tsp Sichuan chilli oil
1 tsp sesame oil
3 tbsp Chinese sesame paste or peanut butter
2 tbsp chicken stock
1 tbsp light soy sauce
1 tbsp Chinese black vinegar
½ tsp Sichuan pepper or black pepper, ground
400 g (14 oz) fresh egg noodles
2 spring onions, finely chopped

Mix peanut oil with grated ginger and sugar. Blanch bean sprouts in a pot of boiling water for 30 seconds. Drain, rinse and set aside.

Toast sesame seeds in a dry pan just until they start to turn brown. Crush lightly.

Mix the oil and ginger mixture with chilli oil, sesame oil, sesame paste, stock and toasted sesame seeds until ingredients are amalgamated. Add soy sauce, vinegar and pepper.

Cook noodles in plenty of boiling water for about 1 minute. Rinse, drain and arrange on a large platter. Pour sauce over the top and scatter with bean sprouts and spring onion.

Serves four.

China – Sichuan   *Noodle i-d 2*

Sichuan noodle-shop noodles

A favourite street-food dish from the noble province of Sichuan, and a great party dish. To turn it into something special, all you need is a pile of disposable chopsticks and a stack of those cute little Chinese takeaway boxes they are always munching from on American television.

6 dried shiitake mushrooms, soaked in warm water for 30 minutes
6 tbsp bamboo shoots
500 g (1 lb) Hokkien noodles
2 tbsp peanut oil
12 fresh straw mushrooms or button mushrooms, finely sliced
1 tsp chilli oil
2 tbsp light soy sauce
1 tbsp shaohsing rice wine, or dry sherry
1 tsp ground Sichuan peppercorns
2 tbsp dried shrimp, soaked in water for 30 minutes
2 spring onions, green part only, finely sliced

Drain shiitake mushrooms, remove stems and cut caps in half. Cut bamboo shoots into thin matchsticks. Pour boiling water over noodles in a large heatproof bowl and let stand for 1 minute. Drain.

Heat peanut oil in a hot wok and cook bamboo shoots, shiitake and fresh mushrooms, noodles and chilli oil for 2 to 3 minutes. Add soy sauce, rice wine, pepper and drained shrimp and cook for 1 minute. Serve on a large warmed platter or in Chinese bowls, scattered with spring onion.

Serves four.

Sichuan beef noodle soup

This is not the world's daintiest, most elegant soup. It's meaty, chunky, spicy, with an in-your-face belt of chilli that lingers in the mouth like a sultry, warm wind. When you've had a bowl of this, you really know you've eaten.

500 g (1 lb) stewing beef
2 tbsp peanut oil
4 slices fresh ginger, cut into matchsticks
3 cloves of garlic, finely chopped
2 tbsp chilli bean paste
2 tbsp shaohsing rice wine, or dry sherry
2 tbsp dark soy sauce
1 tbsp sugar
1 litre (2 pts) chicken stock
1.5 litres (3 pts) water
1 star anise
400 g (14 oz) fresh egg noodles
1 spring onion, finely chopped
a little white pepper
1 tsp sesame oil

Cut beef into bite-size cubes, roughly 2.5 cm (1 inch) square.

In a saucepan, heat oil and stir fry ginger and garlic for 20 seconds, then add beef and stir fry for 2 to 3 minutes. Add chilli bean paste, rice wine, soy sauce, sugar, stock, water and star anise, and cover. Gently simmer for 2½ hours, until beef is tender.

Cook noodles in boiling water for about 1 minute. Drain, then divide among 4 large soup bowls. Ladle some beef and soupy sauce over the top. Add spring onion, white pepper and sesame oil.

Serves four.

Sichuan fish noodles

Being totally landlocked, Sichuan hasn't produced a lot of fish recipes, and the few that exist usually call for freshwater fish. But this dish works swimmingly with ocean fish, especially deep-flavoured, firm-fleshed fish. Be warned, the chilli bean paste is pretty fiery stuff.

250 g (8 oz) fillets of firm white-fleshed fish
2 tsp cornflour
1 egg white
2 tbsp shaohsing rice wine, or dry sherry
3 tbsp peanut oil
100 g (3 oz) water chestnuts, finely chopped
50 g (2 oz) bamboo shoots, cut into matchsticks
2 spring onions, green part only, finely sliced
1 clove of garlic, finely chopped
1 tbsp grated fresh ginger
1 tbsp chilli bean paste
1 tbsp dark soy sauce
1 cup chicken stock
400 g (14 oz) fresh egg noodles

Cut fish into small bite-size pieces and mix with cornflour, egg white and 1 tablespoon rice wine. Heat 2 tablespoons oil in a hot wok and stir fry fish for 1 minute. Pour in any remaining marinade and remaining rice wine. Add water chestnuts and bamboo shoots and stir fry for a further 30 seconds.

Remove the fish mixture, give the wok a quick wipe, then heat the remaining 1 tablespoon oil and stir fry spring onion, garlic and ginger for 20 seconds. Add bean paste, soy sauce and chicken stock. Cook, stirring, for 1 minute, then return fish mixture to the pan. Stir well.

Meanwhile, cook egg noodles in a pot of boiling water for 1 minute. Drain well, add noodles to the wok and toss well to heat through. Serve on a warmed serving platter or in Chinese bowls.

Serves four.

Cross the bridge noodles

In this updated version of the Yunan classic, I have dispensed with the layer of chicken fat on top (Crossing the brige, page 182), and instead, I briefly heat everything on the stove in a serving pot and serve the soupy noodles at the table. Another way would be to place the pot on a portable gas table stove and put everything into the pot while the stock is boiling, then turn off the heat. If, of course, you are taking it to an errant scholar, put the layer of chicken fat on top.

300 g (10 oz) fresh egg noodles
200 g (7 oz) king (large) prawns
1 chicken breast, skinned
200 g (7 oz) fresh white fish fillet
½ bunch choy sum (flowering cabbage)
2 litres (3½ pts) chicken stock
1 tsp finely chopped ginger
1 tsp shaohsing rice wine, or dry sherry
1 tsp soy sauce
1 tsp salt
1 tsp sugar

Cook noodles in plenty of boiling water for 1 minute. Drain and rinse under cold running water; drain well. Set aside, covered, until needed.

Peel prawns and devein by hooking out the black intestinal tract with a fine bamboo skewer. Slice prawns finely on the diagonal. Finely slice chicken breast and fish fillet on the diagonal. Blanch choy sum stems and leaves for 1 minute in simmering water, drain, refresh in cold water, drain again and set aside.

Heat chicken stock in a large clay pot, sand pot or a flameproof casserole dish attractive enough to take to the table. Add ginger, rice wine, soy sauce, salt and sugar and bring to the boil. Add the prepared chicken and fish, and simmer for 4 to 5 minutes, skimming, if necessary. Add noodles, prawns and cabbage and heat through. Remove from the heat, bring to the table and serve in small Chinese bowls.

Serves four.

Bang bang chicken noodles

Traditionally, this popular dish from northern China – of poached chicken in a nutty, sweet, chilli sauce – doesn't include noodles. Yet the subtle crunch of the bean thread vermicelli adds substance and character, and lightens a meat-heavy dish. I think it's an improvement.

200 g (7 oz) bean thread vermicelli
2 tsp sesame oil
1 chicken, about 1.2 kg (2½ lb)
2 spring onions, green part only, finely sliced

Sauce
1 tsp sesame seeds
2½ tbsp Chinese sesame paste or smooth peanut butter
1 tbsp chilli bean sauce
2 tbsp cooked peanut oil (heated, then cooled)
2 tsp sesame oil
1 tbsp sugar
1 tbsp soy sauce
1½ tbsp Chinese black vinegar
2 tbsp chicken stock

Pour boiling water over noodles in a heatproof bowl and let stand for 3 to 5 minutes. Drain. Cut noodles roughly with a pair of scissors and toss with 1 teaspoon sesame oil.

Lightly toast sesame seeds in a dry, hot pan.

Make sauce by combining sesame paste, chilli bean sauce, cooked peanut oil and sesame oil until it forms a paste. Stir in sugar, soy sauce, black vinegar and chicken stock, and sprinkle sesame seeds on top. Set aside.

Put chicken in a saucepan with a snug-fitting lid and just cover with cold water. Remove chicken and bring water to the boil. Return chicken to the water, reduce heat until water is barely simmering, and cover tightly. Simmer for 30 minutes.

Remove chicken from the saucepan and plunge into a large bowl of icy-cold water. Lift out and replunge three or four times, which will give the chicken a marvellously smooth texture. Brush chicken with remaining teaspoon sesame oil. Remove chicken meat from bones and shred finely.

Put noodles on a large serving plate. Arrange shredded chicken on top, and pour on the sauce, serving any extra sauce in a small bowl for dipping. Scatter with spring onion and serve.

Serves four.

Chicken noodle salad

This is a glorious celebration of fresh, wild, garden smells, laced with the heady fragrance of sesame and ginger. It is important to use the chicken soon after it has been cooked. If it has been refrigerated, it will lose much of its lusciousness and bounce, thus losing the point of the whole exercise.

300 g (10 oz) dried rice vermicelli
1 tbsp sesame oil
1 white cut (poached) chicken (from Chinese barbecued meats shop)
1 cucumber
1 small bunch coriander

Dressing
1 bunch spring onions
8 tbsp peanut oil
2 tbsp shredded fresh ginger
1 tsp salt

Pour boiling water over noodles and leave to stand for 6 to 7 minutes. Drain, then transfer to a saucepan of boiling water and cook for one more minute. Rinse in cold water and drain thoroughly. Chop noodles roughly a couple of times with scissors. Add sesame oil and toss thoroughly. Cover and set aside.

Remove meat from the chicken and slice finely, discarding skin and bones.

Peel cucumber, cut in half lengthwise and scoop out seeds with a teaspoon. Slice cucumber flesh lengthwise and cut each slice into thin matchsticks. Pick the leaves from the coriander and set aside.

To make spring onion dressing, finely chop green parts of the spring onions. Gently warm peanut oil in a wok, then add ginger and salt. Stir briefly until salt dissolves, add spring onion and stir for 10 to 15 seconds, until it starts to soften. Remove from heat.

In a bowl, combine chicken, cucumber, noodles, coriander and half the warm dressing. Top with the rest of the dressing.

Serves four.

Dry-cooked green beans with noodles

Spicy green beans are very much the bridesmaids of Sichuan cooking, their main purpose in life being to support the bigger, flashier dishes, and to provide a balanced contrast to meatier offerings. But if you add a little pork and quite a few noodles, the dish suddenly becomes totally self-sufficient.

200 g (7 oz) fresh egg noodles
1½ tsp Sichuan chilli oil (see Basics, page 189)
1 tsp sesame oil
200 g (7 oz) minced pork
1 tbsp light soy sauce
½ tsp cornflour
1 tsp sugar
salt
½ tsp pepper
500 g (1 lb) snake beans, or green beans
3 tbsp peanut oil
2 cloves of garlic, crushed with the side of a knife blade
1 tbsp shaohsing rice wine, or dry sherry

Cook noodles in water at a rolling boil for 1 minute. Drain, rinse in cold water and drain thoroughly. Add 1 teaspoon chilli oil and sesame oil, mix well and set aside.

Mix pork with soy sauce, cornflour, sugar, salt and pepper and set aside.

Cut tips off snake beans and cut into 15 cm (6 in) lengths. Cook in simmering, salted water for 2 minutes, drain and cool under cold running water.

Heat 1 tablespoon peanut oil in a hot wok and stir fry beans with a pinch of salt for 1 minute, until they start to wrinkle. Transfer to a bowl and keep warm.

Reheat wok with remaining 2 tablespoons peanut oil and the garlic. When hot, discard garlic, add pork mixture and stir fry quickly for 3 minutes until it darkens. Add rice wine and ½ teaspoon chilli oil to taste and stir through. Add noodles to the wok, toss well and heat through for 1 to 2 minutes. Tip noodles onto a warmed serving platter and arrange beans on top.

Serves 4 as a side dish.

China – Modern　　　　　　*Noodle i-d* **2**

Gung Bao chicken with Shanghai noodles

Guizhou, a province just south of Sichuan, is known for two things: *mao tai*, a grain spirit that out-proofs vodka, and the almost-as-powerful *gung bao* chicken. Created for a visiting Sichuanese official at the end of the Ching dynasty, this is a spicy, adventure playground of a dish, that becomes a little more approachable with the addition of noodles.

1 chicken, about 1 kg (2 lb)
1 egg white
2 tsp cornflour
3 tbsp peanut oil
6 dried red chillies
2 slices ginger, cut into matchsticks
2 cloves of garlic, crushed
2 tbsp chilli bean sauce
2 tbsp soy sauce
1 tbsp shaohsing rice wine
1 tsp white vinegar
½ tsp salt
1 tsp sesame oil
2 tsp sugar
2 spring onions, cut into 2.5 cm (1 in) lengths
400 g (14 oz) fresh Shanghai noodles
1 tbsp fried peanuts

Remove meat from the chicken and cut into small bite-size cubes. Mix with egg white and cornflour and leave for 15 minutes. Heat 2 tablespoons peanut oil in a hot wok and stir fry chicken for 3 to 4 minutes. Remove chicken and heat remaining oil. Add chillies, ginger and garlic and stir fry for about 30 seconds. Add bean sauce, soy sauce, shaohsing and vinegar, and cook for a further 30 seconds. Add salt, sesame oil, chicken, sugar and spring onion and stir through.

Cook noodles in a pot of water at a rolling boil for 4 to 5 minutes, drain and place on a large warmed serving platter. Top with chicken and sauce and sprinkle with peanuts.

Serves four.

Noodles with pork and pickles

Fresh mustard cabbage or *gai choy* is often used in simple homely soups, but the vegetable achieves an almost noble status in Shanghai when it is pickled in vinegar or preserved in salt, in much the same way as German sauerkraut. Pickled mustard cabbage is often sold with its pickling liquid in large plastic bags. Combine with a little pork and a lot of noodles, and a state of bliss will follow presently.

3 tbsp peanut oil
2 tbsp soy sauce
2 tsp sugar
2 tsp cornflour
½ tsp salt
400 g (14 oz) pork loin, cut into thin slices
400 g (14 oz) Hokkien noodles
1 tsp sesame oil
120 g (4 oz) pickled mustard cabbage
200 g (7 oz) bamboo shoots, cut into thin matchsticks
3 tbsp chicken stock

Combine 1 tablespoon peanut oil, soy sauce, sugar, cornflour and salt in a bowl and stir pork through. Set aside for 30 minutes.

Pour boiling water over noodles in a heatproof bowl and let stand for 30 seconds. Quickly drain and rinse in cold water. Drain again, mix with sesame oil and set aside.

Rinse pickled cabbage in cold water. Dry well with paper towels and shred finely.

Heat 1 tablespoon peanut oil in a hot wok and stir fry bamboo shoots for 30 seconds. Add pickled cabbage and cook for another 30 seconds. Transfer vegetables to a bowl. Heat remaining 1 tablespoon oil and stir fry pork for about 3 minutes until well-coloured. Add stock, bamboo shoots and pickled vegetables and stir fry for 1 or 2 minutes.

Add noodles and toss well to heat through for 1 minute, then serve on a large warmed serving platter or in small Chinese bowls.

Serves four.

Eight treasure noodles

To the Chinese, eight is a significant and lucky number because the word for eight sounds very much like the word for prosperous. For this reason, celebratory banquets will often officially consist of eight courses (even if a few extras are thrown in for good measure). In Chinese cooking, there is eight treasure duck, eight treasure chicken and eight treasure rice, but as far as I know, there have been no eight treasure noodles, until now.

3 tbsp dried shrimp, soaked for 30 minutes
6 dried shiitake mushrooms, soaked for 30 minutes
2 tbsp peanut oil
2 lup cheong sausages, thinly sliced
½ cup lotus seeds or gingko nuts (available canned)
½ onion, finely diced
½ cup bamboo shoots, cut into matchsticks
2 tbsp dark soy sauce
½ tsp five spice powder
2 tsp sesame oil
1 tsp salt
100 g (3 oz) char sieu (red roast pork), cut into thin strips
1 cooked chicken thigh, cut into thin strips
1 cup chicken stock
1 tsp cornflour
1 tbsp shaohsing rice wine
300 g (11 oz) dried wheat noodles
2 spring onions, green part only, finely sliced

Drain dried shrimp and mushrooms. Cut off and discard mushroom stems and slice caps finely. Heat peanut oil in a hot wok and stir fry shrimp, mushroom, sausage, lotus seeds, onion and bamboo shoots for 2 minutes. Add soy sauce, five spice powder, sesame oil and salt.

Add pork, chicken and chicken stock and cook, stirring, for 1 minute. Mix cornflour into rice wine and stir into the mixture. Cook for 1 minute until sauce thickens slightly.

Meanwhile, cook noodles in plenty of boiling water for 3 to 4 minutes. Drain and combine with the sauce, tossing well. Serve on a large warmed platter or in small Chinese bowls with spring onion scattered over the top.

Serves four.

San choy bau with cellophane noodles

With its minced meat, water chestnuts, mushrooms and bamboo shoots inside a crisp, fresh lettuce leaf, san choy bau manages to roll up all the principles of Chinese cooking in one neat little parcel. A relatively recent Hong Kong invention, it is universally loved for its multitude of textures, moving from crisp to soft to crunch. So I hope nobody will mind if I add one more texture in the form of noodles.

50 g (2 oz) bean thread vermicelli
2 fresh quails
6 dried shiitake mushrooms, soaked
3 tbsp peanut oil
2 slices ginger, finely chopped
200 g (7 oz) bamboo shoots, finely chopped
1 clove of garlic, finely chopped
6 water chestnuts, finely chopped
150 g (5 oz) minced pork or chicken
1 slice leg ham, diced
1 tsp sugar
½ tsp salt
pinch of white pepper
1 tbsp dark soy sauce
1 tbsp hoisin sauce
1 tbsp shaohsing rice wine, or dry sherry
2 tbsp chicken stock
1 tsp cornflour, mixed with 1 tsp water
½ tsp sesame oil
8 perfect lettuce leaves, washed and dried

Put noodles in a heatproof bowl and pour boiling water over to cover. Leave for 3 to 4 minutes. Drain, rinse under cold water and drain well. With a pair of scissors, cut into roughly 5 cm (2 in) lengths.

Remove meat from quails, chop finely and set aside.

Drain mushrooms, remove and discard stems and finely slice caps. Heat oil in a hot wok and stir fry mushrooms and ginger for 1 minute. Add bamboo shoots, garlic and water chestnuts and stir fry for 30 seconds. Add quail meat, pork or chicken, ham, sugar, salt and pepper and stir fry over high heat for 3 minutes. Add noodles, soy sauce, hoisin sauce, rice wine, chicken stock and cornflour mixture and cook for another minute or two until it starts to thicken. Sprinkle sesame oil on top, spoon into lettuce cups and serve. To eat, roll up the cup and eat with your fingers.

Makes eight.

Suckling pig, jellyfish and noodle salad

Without the noodles, this traditional banquet dish is texture city, running from the sharp crack of the pig skin, to the India rubber chew of the jellyfish and the satisfying crunch of cucumber and celery. With the noodles, it takes on even more bounce.

200 g (7 oz) dried jellyfish
150 g (5 oz) bean thread vermicelli
1 tbsp sesame oil
2 spring onions, green part only
½ cucumber, peeled
1 carrot, peeled
2 stalks of celery
400 g (14 oz) cooked suckling pig (from Chinese barbecued meats shop)
1 tbsp soy sauce
1 tbsp white vinegar
1 tsp sugar

Soak jellyfish in a large pot of water for 24 hours, changing the water 3 or 4 times. Trim each piece of jellyfish then roll up like a piece of carpet. Trim edges and cut into strips about 1 cm (½ in) wide. Dip strips in boiling water, drain and let cool. Pat dry with paper towels.

Pour boiling water over noodles in a heatproof bowl, let stand for 3 to 5 minutes and drain. Mix with sesame oil and set aside.

Cut 1 spring onion into 5 cm (2 in) sections, then cut each section into matchsticks and set aside. Using a teaspoon, scoop out and discard seeds from the cucumber. Cut cucumber, carrot and celery into fine matchsticks. Remove skin from suckling pig and cut into thin shards. Cut flesh into thin strips and toss lightly through the jellyfish with the cucumber, carrot, celery and noodles. Add soy sauce, vinegar, sugar and remaining spring onion, finely chopped, and toss again. Serve on a large, warmed serving platter and scatter the crisp skin and spring onion strips over the top.

Serves four.

Long-life noodles

I was six years old when my grandfather turned sixty. At the time I was far too young to know that I was really only five years old, as a Chinese baby is deemed to be one-year-old already on the day it is born.

In the See Yup province of Southern China where I came from, birthday parties were as rare and as exotic as the little songbirds that accompanied the old men on their Sunday morning business and gossip sessions.

Once a child's 'coming' out birthday party is held, a month after his birth, he has to wait sixty years for his next birthday party, by which time he will have gathered enough wisdom and knowledge and respect to be worthy of such a celebration.

Naturally my memories of my grandfather's party are hazy. I remember the giggles of my brothers and sisters and cousins, and the clucky, excited chatter of my uncles and aunts as they danced around my grandfather, regaling him with the heroic details of his life. I remember red – lots of red – red banners and red lucky packets, red-dyed eggs and red glazed meats. But most of all I remember the long-life noodles, all glossy and gleaming and studded with mushroom and pork and – for a such a special occasion – abalone.

'The longer the noodle, the longer the life,' squawked my auntie Lu as she placed the bowl in front of me. Eagerly, I tugged at a noodle with my chopstick. It kept coming. I pulled harder, and still it kept coming. I stood on my chair and still it kept coming and coming.

The room fell strangely silent as all faces turned towards me. Never had I seen a noodle so long and so magnificent. My grandfather nodded wisely and smiled.

'Chong Leng Poh, it would seem that the heavens have blessed you,' he said with an air of formality that I found strangely unnerving. 'You owe it to the honour of your family name to make the years that have been bestowed upon you fruitful, rich and meaningful.'

My baby brother then dropped his bowl on the floor, and the squawking and the giggling and the clucking resumed, and I could eat my long-life noodle uninterrupted.

As it turned out, the years that followed were indeed fruitful. At thirteen, I was indentured to an uncle who made some of the finest furniture in all of Southern China. I learned my trade well, and delighted in the feel and form of the bamboo and the rosewood that yielded to me like a white poplar in the autumn wind.

As a young man, I found myself in the fledgling colony of Hong Kong, where my skills were to make me a wealthy and respected businessman.

As business flourished, so too did my happiness. I married a beautiful and devoted young woman who came from the neighbouring village to mine, who bore me five brave and strong sons and three beautiful and respectful daughters.

I proceeded through life with the sure-footedness of a deer that had lived in the same forest all its life and knew every leaf, every twig and every breeze.

At my own sixtieth birthday party, I made a speech in which I referred to my life thus far as 'the golden age of Chong Leng Poh', for that was what my sixty years had surely been.

But less than a year later, spring turned to winter. My wife contracted a respiratory disease that the finest physicians in the colony could not fathom, and died within the week. Loneliness and misery set the beat to which my heart and my life then marched.

By eighty-five, I was a lonely man. Business slowed, and dried up like the pebbled bed of a once-mighty river. I pottered around the factory to fill in the time. Plagues and wars had robbed me of four of my children, and those who were left seemed to be drifting into jobs and lives I didn't understand.

At my hundredth birthday, when I should have been surrounded by a large and admiring family, only five people attended.

I spoke quietly about how happy and fulfilled I was, and turned my head so they could not see the lie in my eyes.

Now it is my birthday again. At one hundred and twenty, I feel as if I am in solitary confinement. I have outlived my children and even my grand-children. My happiness has disappeared into the wind.

I am sitting alone at a rosewood table I made when I was thirty-five years old, while my maid, a young and foolish girl of sixteen, prepares my birthday feast.

'Long-life noodles,' she announces with a bright smile and dull eyes. I thank her and prod my chopsticks into the bowl. Out comes a noodle, as short as a twig for a bird's nest.

I know I should be disappointed, but my heart is not heavy. Instead it is singing. Suddenly, the kitchen door flies open and my wife runs on her tiny feet into the room, her arms flung open, her eyes dancing like moon beams.

My furniture master follows her, cradling in his arms my favourite child Kan Meng, a gurgling, happy three-year-old again. People come from every-where, and crowd around the table.

I call to the maid and ask her to bring more food and my finest *mui kwei lu* wine, but she just stands there, looking at me, her eyes filled with fear. It is only then that I notice that she is sobbing.

Japan

Spring rain tempura

Harusame, also known as 'spring rain', are usually served in salads and soups, but they also have the ability to puff up quite dramatically when deep fried. This unusual tempura recipe makes the most of that ability, giving the seafood an almost theatrical appearance.

400 g (14 oz) white fish fillets
12 medium-size prawns
2 green capsicums
120 g (4 oz) plain flour
2 egg whites
100 g (3 oz) harusame
vegetable oil, for deep frying

Dipping sauce
1 cup dashi (see Basics, page 191)
⅓ cup mirin
⅓ cup light soy sauce
2 tbsp grated daikon (white radish)

Cut fish into 15 cm (6 in) long pieces. Devein prawns by hooking out the black intestinal tract with a fine bamboo skewer. Cut capsicum lengthwise into 2.5 cm (1 in) strips. Put flour in a shallow bowl. Beat egg whites until frothy, but not stiff and peaky. Put noodles in a large plastic bag and cut into 1 cm (½ in) lengths inside the bag.

To make dipping sauce, combine dashi, mirin and soy sauce in a small saucepan and bring to the boil. Remove from heat and pour into individual bowls, adding a little of the grated daikon.

Pour enough oil for deep frying into a hot wok or saucepan and heat until a cube of bread dances on the surface, turning golden within 5 seconds. Roll prawns, fish and capsicum strips first in flour, then in egg white, then in harusame noodles. Drop pieces of coated fish or prawns into the oil, 3 at a time. The noodles will puff out dramatically. Fry until fish or prawns are cooked and noodles are pale gold. Remove and drain well. Continue the process until all seafood and vegetable pieces are fried. (Whisk the egg white briskly before each dipping to keep it frothy.)

Arrange seafood and vegetables on small serving platters, and serve with dipping sauce.

Serves four.

Chilled somen

An exceptionally refreshing summer dish, this is the zen of cold noodles in a single bowl – pared-back, subtle, yet with intriguing and satisfying layers of flavour. Resist the temptation to overcook the noodles, as they need to retain an almost al dente bite to keep up the diner's interest.

200 g (7 oz) somen
6 dried shiitake mushrooms
1½ cups dashi (see Basics, page 191)
½ cup mirin
5 tbsp soy sauce
1 small cucumber, cut into matchsticks
1 handful of watercress, blanched
2 spring onions, finely chopped
1 tsp prepared wasabi

Put noodles in a pot of boiling water. When water returns to the boil, add ½ cup cold water. When it starts to boil again, add another ½ cup of cold water. After about 2 minutes of cooking, the noodles should be ready. Rinse in plenty of cold water and drain. Refrigerate for about 2 hours.

Soak mushrooms in hot water for an hour, then drain and cut off stems.

To make the dipping sauce, combine dashi, mirin, soy sauce and mushrooms in a saucepan and simmer for 5 minutes. Remove mushrooms and cut in half.

Strain liquid and cool quickly by pouring it into bowl sitting in another bowl filled with iced water. Refrigerate until well-chilled.

Divide noodles among 4 Japanese plates or bowls and top with cucumber strips, a little mound of watercress, 2 mushroom halves and a sprinkling of spring onion. Serve with individual bowls of dipping sauce and a little wasabi for adding to individual taste.

Serves four.

Curry udon

The Japanese have adopted the idea of curry in much the same way they adopted the art of deep frying from the Portuguese, and the art of crumbing from eastern Europe. Curry powder first came to Japan in the late 19th century and, while in no way resembling Indian cookery, Japanese curries have a peculiar charm all their own.

300 g (10 oz) dried udon
2 tbsp peanut oil
2 onions, sliced
350 g (11 oz) boned chicken thigh, cut into bite-size cubes
1 cup green beans, blanched
2 tsp curry powder
4 cups chicken stock
1 tsp sugar
2 tbsp tapioca starch or potato starch
2 spring onions, finely sliced

Put noodles in a pot of boiling water. When water returns to the boil, add 1 cup cold water. When water again returns to the boil, add another cup cold water. Repeat the process another 2 to 4 times, depending on thickness of udon, until the noodles are cooked but still have a little resilience. Drain, rinse in cold water and set aside.

Heat oil in a saucepan and fry onion gently for a couple of minutes. Add chicken and cook for 1 minute, then add beans and cook for another minute. Sprinkle on curry powder and mix in with a wooden spoon. Pour in stock and sugar, bring to the boil and simmer for 3 minutes. Mix tapioca starch with a little water. Drizzle mixture into the pot, stirring thoroughly. Cook until the mixture boils and starts to thicken.

Pour boiling water over noodles in a colander or strainer in the sink. Drain well and distribute warmed noodles among 4 individual bowls. Pour sauce over noodles and scatter with spring onion.

Serves four.

Memories of Shikoku udon

To travel around Shikoku, Japan's southernmost island, is to discover the Japan that existed long before neon signs, mini computers and conveyor-belt sushi. It was here I had my first taste of *kamaboko*, a fish paste so superior that it even tasted delicious at the crack of dawn. It was also my first serious encounter with udon noodles, the proudest product of Kagawa, on the northern coast. This is my homage to these two wonderful creations.

8 dried shiitake mushrooms
275 g (9 oz) dried udon
1 tbsp dried wakame (seaweed)
1 cake Japanese fish cake (kamaboko)
2 spring onions, green part only
5 cakes fresh tofu
1.5 litres (2½ pts) dashi (see Basics, page 191)
4 tbsp light soy sauce
3 tbsp mirin
2 tsp sugar
4 hard-boiled eggs, sliced but kept in egg shape

Soak mushrooms in hot water for 1 hour. Drain, remove stems, slice each cap into 3 or 4 strips and set aside.

Place noodles in a pot of boiling water. When water comes back to the boil add 1 cup of cold water. When water returns to the boil, add another cup of cold water. Repeat the process once or twice until noodles are soft, but not sloppy. Rinse in plenty of cold running water, drain and set aside.

Soak wakame in lukewarm water and leave to swell for about 15 minutes. Drain and set aside. Cut fish cake into thin slices. Slice spring onions into 6 cm (2½ in) lengths. Drain tofu cakes, cut each into 12 even cubes and set aside.

Bring dashi to the boil with soy sauce, mirin and sugar. Add mushrooms and tofu and simmer for 5 minutes. Add fish cake slices and simmer for 3 to 4 minutes. Add wakame and spring onion and heat through.

Rinse noodles with boiling water to heat them, drain thoroughly and distribute among 4 large soup bowls. Ladle soup over noodles, including the fish cake, wakame, tofu and mushrooms. Arrange a sliced egg on top of each bowl, fanning out the slices, and serve immediately with chopsticks and spoons.

Serves four.

Japan   *Noodle i-d 13*

Fox noodles with chicken and mushrooms

The Japanese name of this dish – kitsune udon – translates as fox noodles, apparently because of the wily beast's fondness for fried tofu. I don't think this assertion has ever been scientifically proved, but it's such a nice story, I'm prepared to go along with it. This is done in the Osaka style, which just means it has chicken in it. Aburage, fried dried sheets of tofu, are available frozen from Japanese supermarkets.

4 sheets aburage (fried dried tofu sheets)
300 g (10 oz) chicken, cut into 2.5 cm (1 in) squares
8 dried shiitake mushrooms, soaked and stems removed
250 g (8 oz) dried udon
2 spring onions, finely sliced

Simmering broth
500 ml (16 fl oz) dashi (see Basics, page 191)
2 tbsp soy sauce
1 tbsp sugar

Noodle broth
1.5 litres (2½ pts) dashi (see Basics, page 191)
2 tbsp soy sauce
1 tbsp mirin
½ tsp salt
1 tsp sugar

Cut each aburage sheet in half on the diagonal to create 8 triangles. Pour boiling water over aburage to remove the oil, then drain and combine with simmering broth ingredients in a saucepan. Simmer, covered, for 10 minutes, then remove from broth.

In a separate saucepan, combine noodle broth ingredients, bring to the boil and simmer for 2 minutes. Add chicken and mushrooms and simmer for 3 minutes, or until chicken is just cooked through. Skim, if necessary.

Bring a large pot of water to the boil and add noodles. When water returns to the boil, add 1 cup of cold water. When water returns to the boil again, add another cup of cold water, then continue to boil until noodles are one step past al dente (firm, but cooked through).

Drain noodles and rinse with boiling water. Divide among 4 deep soup bowls and pour hot soup on top. Add 2 triangles of aburage to each bowl, along with a little pile of spring onion.

Serves four.

Nabeyaki udon

This dish is often called noodles in a pot, because of the heavy, cast-iron, heat-retaining pot in which the dish is cooked. You'll find these pots at most Japanese food stores, although a heatproof casserole will do the job as well.

4 dried shiitake mushrooms, soaked in hot water for 1 hour
200 g (7 oz) dried udon
2 chicken thighs
4 tbsp soy sauce
3 tbsp mirin
1 tbsp dried wakame (seaweed)
2 large green prawns, peeled and deveined
4 cups dashi (see Basics, page 191)
pinch of salt
1 tbsp sugar
80 g (2¾ oz) Japanese fish cake (kamaboko), finely sliced
vegetable oil, for deep frying
1 cup plain flour
1 quantity tempura batter (see Basics, page 191)
1 egg
1 spring onion, cut into 6 cm (2½ in) lengths

Drain mushrooms, cut off stems and slice caps in half.

Place noodles in a pot of boiling water. When water comes back to the boil, add 1 cup cold water. When water returns to the boil, add another cup of cold water. Repeat once or twice more until noodles are soft, but not sloppy. Rinse in cold running water, drain and set aside.

Cut chicken meat from bone and cut into bite-size pieces. Marinate with 1 tablespoon soy sauce and 1 tablespoon mirin for 30 minutes. Soak wakame in cold water for 10 minutes, drain and set aside.

In a heatproof casserole, combine dashi, remaining soy sauce, remaining mirin, salt and sugar and bring to the boil. Add chicken, mushrooms and fish cake slices and simmer for 15 minutes.

Heat oil in a hot wok until just smoking. Dredge prawns in plain flour, then in the tempura batter and drop straight into the hot oil. Deep fry for about 2 minutes, or until batter turns lightly golden and crisp.

Rinse noodles in boiling water, add to the soup and bring to the boil. Break egg into the soup, add spring onion and wakame and cover for about a minute, cooking over high heat until egg is cooked, but yolk is still runny. Add the 2 tempura prawns and bring pot to the table for sharing. Traditionally, the egg is then broken with chopsticks and stirred through the soup, creating a creamy broth.

Serves two as a meal, or four as part of a meal.

Zaru soba

A zaru is a bamboo basket or slatted bamboo box. Originally, soba were made entirely from buckwheat and were susceptible to breaking, so they were normally steamed then served in the zaru. These days, with the addition of wheat flour, soba are strong enough to withstand boiling. Nevertheless, they are still served in the traditional zaru.

250 g (8 oz) dried soba
500 ml (16 fl oz) dashi (see Basics, page 191)
4 tbsp soy sauce
4 tbsp mirin
½ tsp sugar
1 sheet dried nori (seaweed)
1 tsp wasabi powder, mixed to a paste with a little water
3 spring onions, finely sliced

Bring water to the boil, add soba and when water returns to the boil, add 1 cup cold water. When water again returns to the boil, add another cup cold water. Repeat the process another 2 to 4 times, depending on the thickness of the soba, until the noodles are cooked but still resilient. Rinse thoroughly in cold water and reserve.

Bring dashi, soy sauce, mirin and sugar to the boil, stirring until sugar has dissolved. Cool and chill in refrigerator.

When ready to serve, divide noodles among 4 shallow bowls, or slatted bamboo boxes. Lightly toast nori over a gas flame until crisp, cut with scissors into long, thin strips and scatter over noodles.

Divide chilled dipping sauce among 4 small serving bowls. Each diner picks up some noodles with chopsticks and dips them into the dipping sauce, adding wasabi and spring onion to their personal taste.

Serves four.

Sukiyaki

Although this one-pot beef and vegetable dish is now regarded as Japan's national dish, beef wasn't eaten in Japan until the 1860s, when it was introduced by homesick Westerners. As with most of the ideas the Japanese 'borrowed' from the West, they simply forgot to give it back. Steamed rice and pickles are generally served toward the end of the meal.

150 g (5 oz) fresh silken tofu
8 dried shiitake mushrooms
200 g (7 oz) shirataki
200 g (7 oz) Chinese cabbage, cut into 4 cm (1½ in) slices
4 spring onions
1 bunch enoki mushrooms
1 onion, thinly sliced
500 g (1 lb) eye fillet or sirloin beef, sliced wafer-thin
4 eggs
100 g (3 oz) piece of beef suet

Sauce
3 tbsp sugar
200 ml (7 fl oz) dashi (see Basics, page 191)
200 ml (7 fl oz) soy sauce
200 ml (7 fl oz) mirin

Cut tofu into 2.5 cm (1 in) cubes. Soak mushrooms in hot water for 1 hour, then drain, remove and discard stems. Drain noodles and cook in a pot of boiling water for 1 to 2 minutes.

Slice cabbage into 4 cm (1½ in) sections and cut each section into 4. Cut spring onions into 5 cm (2 in) pieces. Arrange cabbage, tofu, spring onion, noodles, mushrooms and onion with beef on a large platter.

In a small saucepan, combine sauce ingredients and heat, stirring, until sugar has dissolved. Transfer to a jug. Place a whole egg in each of 4 Japanese bowls. Each diner cracks the egg into his or her bowl and beats it lightly with chopsticks.

Put a sukiyaki pan, or a good, heavy-bottomed iron pan, on a portable table stove (or use an electric frying pan). Rub the bottom of the pan with suet. Add onion and let cook for a few minutes. Add beef slices, a little of all the other ingredients and pour some of the sauce over. Be careful not to let the beef overcook (1 minute is plenty). Each diner then selects a piece of meat or vegetable from the pan, dips it quickly in the egg and eats it. Keep replenishing pan as you go.

Serves four.

Tempura soba

The Japanese love adding crisp tempura to noodle soups. Personally, I like to serve the tempura separately at the table and let each person add it while still crisp and crunchy to the soup, but that's a very un-Japanese thing to do.

8 raw prawns
400 g (14 oz) dried soba
oil, for deep frying
8 scallops
½ capsicum, cut lengthwise into 4 strips
1 quantity tempura batter (see Basics, page 191)
1.5 litres (2½ pts) dashi (see Basics, page 191)
2 tbsp mirin
1 tbsp light soy sauce
1 spring onion, sliced

Peel prawns, but leave tails and heads intact. Devein by hooking out the black intestinal tract with a fine bamboo skewer.

Bring water to the boil, add soba and when water returns to the boil, add 1 cup cold water. When water again returns to the boil, add another cup cold water. Repeat the process another 2 to 4 times, depending on the thickness of the soba, until the noodle is cooked but still resilient. Drain, rinse in cold water and set aside for use.

Heat oil in a hot wok until a cube of bread dances on the surface, turning golden within 5 seconds. Dip each piece of seafood and capsicum into batter and deep fry until a nice, even golden colour. Be sure to drain tempura well on paper towels.

When ready to serve, pour boiling water over noodles in a colander or steamer to heat, and drain well. Bring dashi to the boil in a saucepan, add mirin and soy sauce, and simmer for 2 minutes. Place some noodles in each of 4 deep bowls and add broth just to the top of the noodles. Add tempura pieces and a little spring onion.

Serves four.

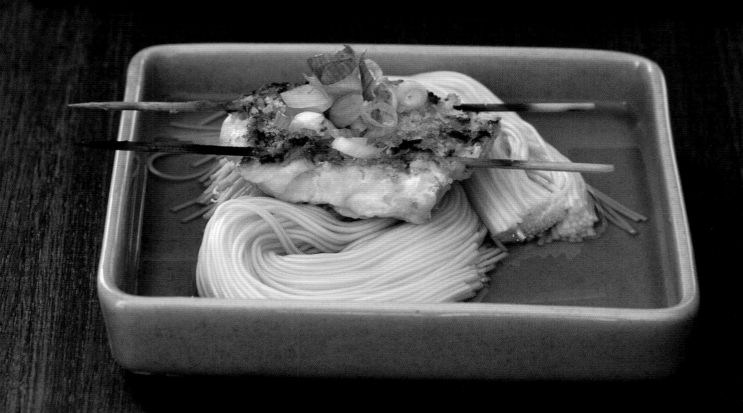

Somen with salt-grilled snapper

The Japanese have a way with salt grilling that tends to give fish and seafood the very breath of the sea. Not only does salt give a distinctive, crisp texture, but it accentuates the integral flavours of the fish. This dish works with practically any fish, particularly oily varieties, as long as they are fresh.

250 g (8 oz) somen
3 cups dashi (see Basics, page 191)
1 tbsp soy sauce
1 tbsp mirin
2 tsp sea salt
½ tsp sugar
6 fresh shiitake mushrooms (optional)
2 skin-on snapper fillets, about 250 g (8 oz) each
sea salt, for grilling
2 spring onions, chopped

Put somen in a pot of boiling water. When water returns to the boil, add ½ cup cold water. When it returns to the boil, add another ½ cup cold water. After about 2 minutes of cooking, noodles should be ready. Rinse well under cold water, drain and set aside.

Bring dashi to the boil with soy sauce, mirin, salt and sugar, add mushrooms and simmer for 3 to 4 minutes. Remove from heat and set aside.

Cut and trim each fillet into 2 neat almost-squares. Thread a bamboo skewer up one side of each square, so that it looks like a flag. Thread another skewer up the other side. This will keep the fillets flat while they grill. Scatter a little sea salt on a chopping board and place fish, skin-side-down, on the salt. Sprinkle a little more salt over the flesh side and leave for 5 minutes. Place on a hot charcoal grill and cook, skin-side-down, until fish is three-quarters done. Turn and cook on the other side for a minute or two.

Remove mushrooms from broth and cut into thin slivers. Pour boiling water through reserved noodles in a strainer to heat.

Divide noodles among 4 shallow bowls, scatter with mushroom slivers and pour hot broth into each bowl. Remove fish from skewers and place over each noodle pile. Scatter with spring onion and serve.

Serves four.

Odamaki mushi

This delicate Japanese custard is traditionally made in pretty, lidded pots, as for *chawan mushi*. Small ramekins (200 ml [7 fl oz]) tightly covered with plastic wrap, won't have the same table theatre, but will work just as well.

4 green prawns, shelled and deveined
pinch of sea salt
1 small chicken breast, cut into 1 cm (½ in) cubes
1 tsp sake
1 tsp soy sauce
4 medium-size eggs
1 tbsp soy sauce
1 tbsp mirin
2¼ cups dashi (see Basics, page 191)
16 cooked udon strands
2 water chestnuts, thinly sliced
2 dried shiitake mushroom caps, soaked and halved
20 enoki mushrooms
1 spring onion, green part only, finely sliced

In two separate bowls, sprinkle prawns with sea salt, and marinate diced chicken in 1 teaspoon each sake and soy sauce. Leave to stand.

Beat eggs lightly in a bowl with a fork, being careful not to let the mixture froth and bubble. Add soy sauce and mirin to the cold dashi and pour liquid into the eggs in a slow, steady stream, gently folding with a wooden spoon as you go. It should be mixed well, but without creating bubbles.

Place a few noodles at the bottom of 4 lidded bowls. Add chicken, prawns, water chestnuts and mushrooms and pour in the egg and dashi mixture to about 1 cm (½ in) from the top. Cover each with a lid and wrap with plastic wrap, or cover ramekins with plastic wrap, and place in a steamer over moderate to high heat for about 20 minutes. Alternatively, set the pots in a baking tray half-filled with water and cook for up to 30 minutes in an oven heated to 220°C (425°F).

When custards are set, but still retain a wobble, they are ready to serve. Top each custard with a little spring onion, replace lids, and serve with Japanese spoons and chopsticks.

Serves four.

Ramen with char sieu

It is ironic to note that the most popular noodles in Japan are not Japanese, but the Chinese-style ramen wheat noodles. This dish borrows again from the Chinese in the form of char sieu, gloriously red roast pork, which you'll find hanging in the window of every Chinese barbecued meat shop.

375 g (12 oz) fresh ramen
250 g (8 oz) char sieu (red roast pork)
2 hard-boiled eggs
24 fresh spinach leaves
1.5 litres (2½ pts) chicken stock
1 tbsp soy sauce
½ tsp sugar
½ tsp salt
8 slices kamaboko fish cake
16 pieces of menma (pickled bamboo shoot)
2 spring onions, finely sliced

Boil noodles in plenty of water for about 2–3 minutes. Rinse in cold water, drain and reserve.

Cut pork and eggs into thin slices. Blanch spinach in boiling water for 10 seconds. Put stock in a saucepan, add soy sauce, sugar and salt and bring to the boil. Add fish cake slices, simmer for 2 minutes and remove.

Pour boiling water over noodles in a strainer to heat. Divide them among 4 large soup bowls and pour stock over. Carefully arrange pork, fish cake, spinach, menma and sliced egg on top. Scatter with spring onion and serve.

Serves four.

Moon-viewing noodles

Of course that's not a mysterious moon drifting meaningfully through the clouds. It's a raw egg. If you can see the beauty in that, too, then you're ready to appreciate *tsukimi udon*, which is a great favourite in a country where moon-viewing is a popular family pastime.

400 g (14 oz) fresh, cooked, or instant udon
1.5 litres (2½ pts) dashi (see Basics, page 191)
1 tablespoon mirin
2 tablespoons light soy sauce
4 fresh eggs
8 slices kamaboko (fish cake)
4 dried shiitake mushrooms, soaked, stems removed, and caps sliced in half
½ sheet nori (seaweed)
2 large spring onions, sliced thinly on the diagonal

Pour boiling water over noodles in a large bowl and gently separate them with chopsticks. Drain, rinse under cold water and drain again.

Bring dashi to the boil in a saucepan with mirin and soy sauce and simmer for 3 minutes. Reheat noodles briefly in boiling water, then divide among 4 warmed serving bowls, making a little hollow nest in each pile.

Add enough boiling stock to come halfway up the noodles, then break an egg into each nest. Arrange fish cake and mushroom to one side and carefully ladle more boiling soup on top to just cover the egg. Immediately cover each bowl with a plate and leave for 2 minutes before removing it.

If you're not sure about eating a very lightly set egg, poach the eggs separately to your liking and slip them in at the last moment. Toast nori over a gas flame for a few seconds until it crisps. Cut into thin strips and scatter over the top, along with the spring onion.

Serves four.

Teriyaki salmon with udon and spinach

The whole idea of teriyaki grilling is devilishly clever. Sugar and sake are added to the basting liquid not just for the distinctive flavour, but to achieve that glamorous glazed look and to encourage those highly desirable scorched brown bits.

2 litres (3½ pts) dashi (see Basics, page 191)
2 tbsp soy sauce
2 tbsp mirin
1 knob of fresh ginger
300 g (10 oz) dried udon
4 small salmon fillets, skinned
1 bunch spinach, washed
4 spring onions, sliced on the diagonal

Teriyaki sauce
2 tbsp dark soy sauce
1 tbsp sake
1 tbsp mirin
1 tsp sugar
1 tbsp peanut oil

For teriyaki sauce, combine dark soy, sake, mirin, sugar and oil in a small pot and heat, stirring, until sugar has dissolved. Set aside.

Heat dashi in a second pot and add soy and mirin. Peel ginger, cut into cubes and crush in a garlic press to get 1 tablespoon ginger juice. Add juice to broth and adjust flavourings to taste.

Cook noodles in plenty of boiling, salted water until al dente, about 8 minutes. Drain and rinse in cold water, cover with plastic wrap and set aside.

Brush salmon with teriyaki sauce and grill quickly on a hot, well-oiled grill, leaving inside lightly pink. Bring broth to just below the boil. Add noodles to dashi for 30 seconds to heat through, then divide noodles among 4 warmed bowls. Dip spinach leaves briefly in broth to wilt them, and distribute among the bowls. Ladle hot broth into each bowl and top noodles with grilled salmon. Scatter spring onion on top and serve with chopsticks and spoons.

Serves four.

Soba with eggplant and miso

We tend to think of eggplant as a Mediterranean vegetable, yet nobody explores its potential more thoroughly or more joyously than the Japanese. The combination of eggplant and red miso is a triumph of compatibility. I'm sure I'm not the first person to think of adding the sweet nuttiness of soba noodles to this traditional pairing, served at room temperature.

300 g (10 oz) dried soba
1 tsp sesame oil
2 medium eggplants
2 tbsp peanut oil
150 ml (5 fl oz) dashi (see Basics, page 191)
3 tbsp red miso
3 tbsp sugar
2 tsp sesame seeds
1 spring onion, finely chopped

Bring water to the boil, add soba, and when water returns to the boil, add 1 cup cold water. When water again returns to the boil, add another cup cold water. Repeat the process 2 to 4 times, depending on the thickness of the soba, until the noodle is cooked, but still resilient. Drain well, mix with sesame oil and set aside.

Wash and trim eggplant and cut into bite-size chunks. Heat peanut oil in a frying pan and cook eggplant, stirring, until the flesh is almost translucent. Add dashi, cover and simmer for 5 minutes. Add a little of the liquid to the miso in a small bowl and whisk well. Stir in sugar and whisk until it dissolves. Dribble this mixture slowly over eggplant, stirring well, and simmer for another minute or two until eggplant is tender and giving.

Put noodles in a strainer or colander and pour boiling water over to heat them. Drain well. Swirl a small handful of noodles on each plate and top with a ladleful of eggplant and sauce. Scatter a few sesame seeds and a little spring onion over the top and serve.

Serves four.

Five mushroom miso with ramen

Ten years ago, this dish would have been impossible to make outside Japan, as the only mushrooms we could lay our hands on were fresh champignons or dried shiitake. Actually, it would still have worked, but it's so much better this way.

400 g (14 oz) fresh ramen
1 tbsp dried wakame (seaweed)
100 g silken tofu
6 cups dashi (see Basics, page 191)
6 tbsp red miso paste
2 tbsp mirin
8 fresh shiitake mushrooms
10 dried shiitake mushrooms, soaked and halved
1 bunch enoki mushrooms, separated
½ cup shimeji mushrooms, separated
4 abalone mushrooms, sliced into thin strips
12 large spinach leaves, stems removed
1 spring onion, green part only, cut into 4 cm (1½ in) lengths

Cook noodles in boiling water for 1 minute, rinse under cold water, drain and reserve. Soak wakame in lukewarm water and leave to swell for around 15 minutes. Drain tofu and cut into 1.5 cm (½ in) cubes.

Bring dashi to the boil in a saucepan. Whisk 2 tablespoons hot dashi into the miso paste in a bowl, and whisk well until blended. Little by little, pour miso back into the dashi, stirring. Add mirin and simmer over low heat for 2 to 3 minutes.

Add tofu and all the mushrooms and cook for 2 or 3 minutes. Add spinach and cook for up to 1 minute, until it wilts. Add wakame.

Pour boiling water over noodles in a colander or strainer to heat through. Drain and distribute noodles among 4 deep serving bowls. Use tongs to distribute wilted spinach leaves among the bowls, then ladle soup and mushrooms over the top. Top each bowl with 3 or 4 lengths of spring onion.

Serves four.

Malaysia

Char kueh teow

There are two secrets to this dish. One is not to crowd your wok – too many noodles and you'll steam more than stir fry. The second is heat. Keep the flame high and the noodles moving, and the dish takes on a dark, almost scorched flavour known as 'the breath of the wok'.

500 g (1 lb) fresh rice sheet noodles
2 tbsp vegetable oil and 1 tsp peanut oil
2 cloves of garlic, crushed with the side of a knife blade
3 dried red chillies, soaked, drained and chopped
12 green prawns, peeled and deveined
200 g (7 oz) squid, cleaned and finely sliced
100 g (3 oz) char sieu (red roast pork), sliced into thin strips
1 lup cheong sausage, steamed and thinly sliced
1 cup bean sprouts, blanched for 30 seconds
2 tbsp dark soy sauce
2 tbsp light soy sauce
1 tbsp oyster sauce
2 eggs, beaten
4 spring onions, finely chopped

Cut noodles into strips 2 cm (¾ in) wide and place in a bowl. Pour boiling water over and gently pull them apart with a pair of chopsticks. Drain immediately and rinse under cold water to prevent overcooking. Drain well and mix with 1 teaspoon of peanut oil to prevent sticking.

Heat remaining oil in a hot wok and stir fry garlic and chilli for 30 seconds. Add prawns, squid, pork and sausage and stir fry for a further 2 minutes over high heat. Add bean sprouts and cook for a further minute. Remove contents from wok and set aside.

Put a little more oil in the wok, if necessary. Add noodles, soy sauce and oyster sauce and toss over high heat for a minute or two, before returning the other ingredients to the wok.

Push noodles to one side of the wok, pour egg in the space created, cover with the noodles and toss to distribute the egg. Scatter with spring onion and serve hot.

Serves four.

Curry mee

Malaysians love to breakfast on this thick, hearty hawker-style curry dish. There is a seafood version using prawns, clams and fish balls, but clams may be a little hard to take at breakfast if you're used to toast and jam.

1 small chicken
1 cup green beans, cut into 5 cm (2 in) lengths
1 tbsp peanut oil
1 tsp grated fresh turmeric, or ½ tsp ground turmeric
1 slice ginger, chopped
1 slice galangal, chopped
2 stalks of lemongrass, white part only, sliced
4 candlenuts or macadamias
6 shallots, roughly chopped
2 dried chillies, soaked overnight, drained and chopped
1 tsp shrimp paste
3 cloves of garlic, chopped
2 cups thick coconut milk
4 fried bean curd puffs, halved diagonally
½ tsp salt
1 tsp sugar
4 cups chicken stock
500 g (1 lb) Hokkien noodles
2 cups bean sprouts
2 hard-boiled eggs, quartered
2 limes, cut into wedges
2 fresh red chillies, sliced
3 tbsp crisp-fried shallots (available from Asian grocery stores)

Remove meat from chicken and chop into bite-size pieces. Blanch green beans in simmering water for 1 minute, refresh in cold water and drain. Heat oil in a non-stick frying pan and fry chicken until it colours a little.

Using a mortar and pestle, pound the turmeric, ginger, galangal, lemongrass, nuts, shallot, chilli, shrimp paste and garlic to a smooth paste. Scoop 3 tablespoons of thick coconut milk off the top and heat in a hot wok. Add curry paste and fry until it smells warm and fragrant. Add chicken pieces, beans, bean curd puffs, salt, sugar, remaining coconut milk and stock, and simmer over low heat until chicken is cooked, about 10 minutes.

Pour boiling water over noodles in a heatproof bowl and let stand for 30 seconds. Drain and distribute noodles among 4 deep soup bowls. Put some bean sprouts on top and ladle chicken and curry over. Serve with egg quarters, lime wedges, red chilli and crisp-fried shallots.

Serves four.

Hokkien mee

This is one of the great standards of Malaysian hawker-stall cooking, with every merchant claiming to have the one, the true, the authentic recipe. There is a popular, darker version of the dish, to which oyster sauce and dark soy are added, but I prefer this lighter variation, which gives the subtle flavours of the squid and prawn a chance to star.

200 g (7 oz) fresh Hokkien egg noodles
100 g (3 oz) rice vermicelli
200 g (7 oz) squid, cleaned
3 tbsp peanut oil
2 eggs, beaten
2 cloves of garlic, crushed with the side of a knife blade
12 raw prawns, peeled
100 g (3 oz) char sieu (red roast pork), diced
2 cups bean sprouts, washed
1 cup hot chicken stock, or stock made from prawn shells
2 tbsp light soy sauce

Pour boiling water over Hokkien noodles in a heatproof bowl, leave for a minute, then drain and rinse. Pour boiling water over rice vermicelli in a heatproof bowl and leave to stand for 6 to 7 minutes. Rinse under cold water, drain and set aside.

Cut squid into 2.5 cm (1 in) squares and score lightly with the tip of a knife.

Heat 1 tablespoon oil in a hot wok and swirl around to coat the surface. Pour in beaten egg and quickly swirl around the pan to form a thin omelette. When cooked on one side, gently separate the edge of the omelette from the wok with a knife. Place a plate over the wok and invert the whole thing so that the omelette drops onto the plate. Slide the omelette back in and quickly cook the other side. Roll up into a tight roll and slice across into thin strips.

Heat remaining oil in the hot wok and stir fry garlic for 1 minute. Add squid and prawns and stir fry for 2 minutes. Add pork, egg strips and bean sprouts and stir fry for a minute. Add noodles, stock and soy sauce and toss through for a minute or two.

Serves four.

Indian mee goreng

The great thing about multicultural Malaysia is that every ethnic group gets a chance to influence the local cuisine. This dish came from the Indian street vendors who gave their own unique twist to the Chinese noodle that was adopted by the local Malays as their own. Don't even think about trying to find this dish in India.

400 g (14 oz) fresh Hokkien egg noodles
2 tbsp vegetable oil
1 onion, sliced
½ cup bean sprouts
2 boiled potatoes, cut into small cubes
2 tomatoes, cut into small cubes
2 tbsp tomato sauce (ketchup)
1 tbsp sweet chilli sauce (Lingham's)
1 cup small fresh shrimp, cooked
2 squares dried bean curd cake (taukwa), cut into cubes
salt and sugar, to taste
1 egg, beaten
2 spring onions, sliced
½ cup shredded lettuce
1 lime, quartered
2 tbsp crisp-fried shallots (available from Asian grocery stores)

Pour boiling water over noodles, drain, rinse and set aside.

Heat oil in a hot wok and fry onion until soft. Add noodles and cook for 2 minutes. Add bean sprouts, potato, tomato, tomato sauce, chilli sauce, shrimp and bean curd cake and cook over high heat, stirring, until well mixed. Add salt and sugar to taste.

Tilt wok, push noodles to one side, pour in egg, cover with noodles and leave to set for 30 seconds. Toss well, add spring onion and toss again. Serve topped with shredded lettuce, lime wedges and crisp-fried shallots.

Serves four.

Mee rebus

Sweet potato might not be the first ingredient that pops into your mind when you think about making a sauce for noodles, but when Malay hawker stall cooks use it to thicken this full-on gravy, the results are nothing short of miraculous.

5 candlenuts or macadamias, crushed
6 shallots, chopped
2 slices of fresh ginger, shredded
2 cloves of garlic, chopped
3 dried red chillies, chopped
2 slices galangal, chopped
1 tbsp Malaysian curry powder
2 tbsp dried shrimp, ground to a powder
2 tbsp peanut oil
300 g (10 oz) good beef (e.g. fillet), sliced thinly
2 tsp sugar
2 tbsp yellow bean sauce (taucheo)
1 cup of boiled sweet potato, mashed
2½ cups beef stock
400 g (14 oz) fresh Hokkien noodles
200 g (7 oz) bean sprouts, scalded in boiling water
2 tbsp crisp-fried shallots (available from Asian grocery stores)
2 red chillies, finely sliced
2 pieces hard beancurd (taukwa), deep fried and sliced
1 cucumber, cut into thin slices
2 spring onions, green part only, sliced finely
2 hard-boiled eggs, quartered

Using a mortar and pestle, pound candlenuts, shallot, ginger, garlic, chilli, galangal, curry powder and shrimp powder to a thick paste. Heat peanut oil in a hot wok and fry paste until it is warmly fragrant. Add beef and cook for 2 minutes. Add sugar and yellow bean sauce, stir through, then add sweet potato and stock. Mix well.

Cover noodles with boiling water in a heatproof bowl. Leave to stand for 30 seconds, then drain. Put some noodles and beansprouts in each of 4 large individual bowls and pour on the gravy. Top with crisp-fried shallots, a little sliced chilli, beancurd slices, some cucumber, spring onion and hard-boiled egg quarters.

Serves four.

Mee Siam

Created by Nonya Malaysian cooks inspired by the noodle dishes of Thailand. With its nice, sweet-salty flavours, it winds up being neither Thai nor Malaysian, but something that forms a bridge of good taste between the two.

300 g (10 oz) dried rice vermicelli
1 tbsp shallots, finely chopped
10 dried red chillies, soaked, drained and chopped
1 tbsp belacan (shrimp paste)
2 tbsp dried shrimp, ground to a powder
3 tbsp peanut oil
250 g (8 oz) fresh prawns, peeled and deveined
1 cup water
1 tsp salt
1 tbsp sugar
1 tsp oyster sauce
2 cups bean sprouts

Sauce
4 tbsp yellow bean sauce (taucheo), lightly mashed
2 tbsp sugar
1 onion, finely sliced
2 tbsp tamarind water (see Glossary, page 197)
3 cups coconut milk

To serve
3 hard-boiled eggs, quartered
2 limes, quartered
1 tbsp crisp-fried shallots (available from Asian grocery stores)
2 spring onions, cut into short lengths

Pour boiling water over noodles and leave for 4 to 5 minutes. Rinse in cold water, drain and set aside. Pound or blend shallot, chilli, belacan and shrimp powder to a fine paste. Heat oil in a hot wok and fry prawns for 1 minute. Remove prawns, then add paste and fry until it is fragrant. Reserve half the paste.

Add water, salt, sugar and oyster sauce to the wok and bring to the boil, stirring. Add bean sprouts and cook for 1 minute. Add noodles and cook for 3 to 4 minutes until liquid is absorbed.

For the sauce, blend soy beans, sugar, onion, tamarind water and coconut milk in a pot, and bring to the boil, stirring. Add reserved paste and oil and simmer for 5 minutes.

Arrange noodles on a large platter and drizzle with hot sauce. Surround with eggs, prawns and lime wedges and sprinkle with shallots and spring onion.

Serves four.

Penang laksa

When most people think of laksa, they think of curry laksa, or laksa lemak. But the people of Penang have devised their own laksa using fish. Rather than thick, creamy and coconutty, this laksa is sour and brothy – a totally different kettle of fish.

4 cups cold water
½ tsp salt
500 g (1 lb) blue mackerel, or other firm-fleshed fish
2 cups tamarind water (see Glossary, page 197)
2 stalks of lemongrass, white part only, finely sliced
2 tsp ground turmeric
1 tbsp belacan (shrimp paste)
6 dried chillies, soaked, drained and chopped
2 cm (¾ in) piece galangal or ginger, finely chopped
1 tbsp palm sugar, or white sugar
300 g (10 oz) round rice noodles or Hokkien noodles
1 cucumber, peeled, seeded and cut into thin matchsticks

Bring water and salt to the boil, add fish and simmer for 5 minutes. Remove fish, cool, then flake off flesh with your hands and set aside. Return heads and bones to the water. Add tamarind water and simmer for a further 10 minutes, then strain through a fine sieve and set stock aside.

Pound or blend lemongrass, turmeric, belacan, chilli and galangal to a paste. Add to fish stock with sugar and simmer for 10 minutes. Add fish and heat through.

Pour boiling water over noodles in a heatproof bowl. Drain and divide noodles among 4 warm serving bowls. Add soup and top with cucumber.

Serves four.

Malaysia   *Noodle i-d 9*

Laksa lemak

This is my number one, very favourite noodle dish in all the world. It has every taste sensation you can think of – tart, salty, sour, sweet, rich, tangy, creamy – and a few others they haven't invented words for yet. While you can buy some perfectly good prepared laksa pastes these days, you never get the same feeling of having really earned your laksa as when you pound the paste yourself.

2 tbsp vegetable oil
1 quantity laksa paste (see Basics, page 190) or 4 tbsp bought paste
1.5 litres (2½ pts) chicken stock
2 tsp palm or brown sugar
1 tsp salt
2 cups coconut milk
300 g (10 oz) fresh round rice noodles
   or 200 g (7 oz) Hokkien noodles and 100 g (3 oz) rice vermicelli
meat from half a cooked chicken, sliced
8 fish balls
8 raw prawns, peeled
4 squares fried bean curd puffs, cut in half diagonally
2 tbsp bamboo shoots, rinsed and cut into matchsticks
1 cucumber, peeled, seeded and cut into matchsticks
1 cup bean sprouts, blanched
fresh mint and coriander sprigs, for garnish

Heat oil in a hot wok and fry laksa paste for about 5 minutes until fragrant. Add stock, sugar and salt and bring to the boil. Reduce heat and add coconut milk, stirring constantly as it heats.

Pour boiling water over rice noodles in a heatproof bowl. Drain and rinse. (Alternatively, pour boiling water over Hokkien noodles. Drain and rinse. Cook rice vermicelli in plenty of water at a rolling boil for about 2 minutes. Drain.)

Add chicken, fish balls, prawns, bean curd puffs and bamboo shoots, and heat through for the last couple of minutes cooking time, without boiling.

Distribute noodles among 4 deep bowls. Using tongs, distribute fish balls, prawns and chicken among the bowls and top with hot soup. Scatter cucumber and bean sprouts on top along with sprigs of mint and coriander.

Serves four.

Malaysia   *Noodle i-d **9***

Singapore beehoon

Singapore noodles, or Sing chow, is widely known outside the Lion City, but unheard of in its home town. More usually it is simply called fried beehoon, after the noodle itself. The popular addition of curry powder is not to my taste, but feel free to add a teaspoon worth of good, fresh Malaysian curry powder if it is to yours.

250 g (8 oz) rice vermicelli
1 tbsp vegetable oil
½ onion, or 4 shallots, sliced
1 egg, lightly beaten
1 tbsp chicken stock or water
100 g (3 oz) cooked shredded chicken
100 g (3 oz) char sieu (red roast pork), sliced
1 tbsp dark soy sauce
1 tbsp light soy sauce
150 g (5 oz) prawns, shelled
½ cup bean sprouts
2 spring onions, finely chopped
½ cup shredded lettuce
1 tbsp crisp-fried shallots (available from Asian grocery stores)
1 lemon, quartered

Pour boiling water over noodles in a heatproof bowl and let stand for 6 to 7 minutes. Rinse in cold water, and drain.

Heat oil in a hot wok and fry onion until it starts to soften. Add egg and stir until softly cooked. Add drained noodles and stir constantly to coat with egg. Moisten with a little stock and cook for 1 minute, then add chicken, pork and soy sauces and cook for 2 minutes. Add prawns and cook for 1 minute. Add bean sprouts and spring onion and cook for another minute or two. Serve on a large warmed platter, topped with shredded lettuce, crisp-fried shallots and lemon wedges for squeezing over the lot.

Serves four.

Chilli prawn noodles

Traditionally, Singapore's famous, finger-licking chilli crab and chilli prawn dishes are mopped up with slices of fresh, commercial white bread. In this dish, the luscious sweet/spicy sauce comes with its own inbuilt mopping-up agent in the form of Hokkien noodles. While not strictly authentic, it is strictly delicious.

500 g (1 lb) green (raw) prawns, unpeeled
2 tbsp peanut oil
2½ cups chicken stock
1 clove of garlic, crushed with the side of a knife blade
2 tbsp sweet chilli sauce (e.g. Lingham's SOS brand)
4 tbsp tomato sauce or ketchup
½ tsp salt
1 tsp sugar
1 tsp cornflour, blended with 1 tbsp cold water
4 spring onions, chopped
1 egg white, beaten
400 g (14 oz) fresh Hokkien noodles

Devein prawns by hooking out the black intestinal tract with a fine bamboo skewer. Heat peanut oil in a hot wok and fry prawns for 1 to 2 minutes until they turn red. Add chicken stock and simmer for 1 minute. Add garlic, chilli sauce, tomato sauce, salt and sugar, and stir well to mix.

Add cornflour paste, bring to boil and stir for 1 minute. Add half the spring onion and toss well. Slowly dribble egg white into the sauce (a good trick is to pour it through the tines of a fork), stirring constantly, until the sauce thickens.

Pour boiling water over noodles in a heatproof bowl, leave to stand for 2 minutes and drain. Arrange on a warmed serving platter and pour prawns and sauce on top. Scatter with remaining spring onion.

Serves four.

Malaysia – Modern   *Noodle i-d 3*   125

Noodle love

Endo Furahashi pushes through the indigo curtain and steps into the little workroom that fronts the bleakness of the Takamatsu street. Tall and thin, in a white chef's outfit, he looks not unlike an udon noodle himself.

He bows a little automatic bow towards the plate glass window, then immediately sets to work mixing the fine white wheat flour with pure, clean Kagawa-prefecture water. Within minutes, a small crowd gathers: a businessman in a shiny blue suit, two white-socked schoolgirls, a mother with a baby cradled loosely in her arms, and Yoshiko, her eyes fixed on the willowy young man in the spotless white jacket. Her stare is intense and unblinking, as if she fears that even a momentary pause would cause the chef to disappear from sight.

Whether or not Furahashi-san is aware that the twenty-year-old hotel clerk has been standing at the window every day for the past three weeks is hard to say, for he rarely acknowledges his audience. Once flour and water are in the young chef's hands, his eyes focus only on his precious udon, and the rest of the world simply has to wait its turn.

So he doesn't notice Yoshiko's little intake of breath as he thrusts his hands into the dough and begins to knead, pushing with the palms, and gathering with the fingers in a kind of sublime culinary sign language.

Yoshiko loves to watch his hands. To her, they are like two strong salmon swimming upstream against a strong white tide. She loves their strength, their sense of purpose, their power. They are the hands of a strangler, an assassin, a conqueror. She also loves the way they caress the smooth satin surface of the finished dough in much the same way that the woman beside her touches the forehead of her baby. They are the hands of an artist, a holy man, a lover.

Alone each night in her bed, she has difficulty remembering his face, or the colour of his eyes, or the shine of his hair. But she knows his hands better than the contours of her own body, and even as sleep closes in around her, she wills herself to stay awake just a little longer to further dwell on the long, strong fingers, the one vein that snakes down the back of the right hand, the clean, broad nails, and the little stitch scar below the left thumb.

To a native of the island of Shikoku, udon chefs are hardly a novelty. Yet, on that morning three weeks ago, as she rushed from the bus stop to the Takamatsu City Hotel where she worked, it was as if the hands were beckoning her to the window.

She watched, mesmerised by their act of creation. When she finally arrived at the hotel, she looked so different, her cheeks flushed and her eyes bright, that the doorman's head turned to watch her go by.

Since then, she has been drawn back every day, timing her arrival or her errands to his udon-making schedule.

Now, the chef picks up the rested dough and with a few flicks of his wooden rolling pin, transforms it into a large white tablecloth. His hands then gently fold the tablecloth over itself in a large S shape and place it on the cutting board as if it were precious silk. He picks up the large steel cutting blade. The index finger of his right hand rubs curiously along the edge of the blade to confirm its sharpness. He slices in a motion so uniform, so controlled and so smooth that it seems barely human. Finally, he gathers up the thick white noodles with the rolling pin, holds them aloft like a matador holding up the ear of a vanquished bull, bows his little automatic bow and disappears through the indigo curtain.

Only Yoshiko and the woman with the baby are still standing on the footpath. The woman nods politely, then whispering soothingly to her baby, walks off down the street. Yoshiko waits a moment, then bounds up the stairs to the first-floor dining-room.

'Sanuki udon?' asks the waiter, using the ancient name for the prefecture of Kagawa now given to the famed local noodles, renowned for their strength and resilience. 'Sanuki udon,' she confirms.

He reappears with a large bowl of noodles floating in a clear, pure dashi broth, flavoured with soy and mirin. It sits on the table, steaming like the hot springs of Shionoe.

Yoshiko bends over the bowl as if praying. Her slight body moves with the rhythm of her breath. She then snaps her chopsticks in two, and toys playfully with the noodles, watching as they slip and slide sinuously, seemingly dancing the *awa odori*, the dance of joy.

She is looking at the noodles, but she is seeing his hands. Picking up a large thick udon strand, she purses her lips and begins to make a loud whooshing sound, as is traditional with the eating of hot udon. But there is something different about her whooshing – something desperate, like an injured animal gasping for breath – that makes two businessmen at the next table stop their own whooshing and stare.

She can't see them. Her eyes are shut tight as she allows the noodle to slide down, feeling his hands on her throat, feeling their two souls meet and mingle like the swirling whirlpools of the Naruta Straits.

She hurries back to work, past the empty workroom. A little light-headed still, she runs around the corner, and straight into the woman with the baby, who clutches the child to her chest instinctively. The baby cries, his little hands opening and closing like oyster shells in the cold air. *His* hands. There are the same long fingers, the same defined knuckles, the same slight flattening around the nail. She gasps, turns and runs.

Thailand

Mee krob 130
Gwaytio neua sap 132
Kao soi 133
Khanom jeen with spicy pork 134
Moo sarong 135
Pad Thai 136
Seafood and glass noodle salad 137
Pad woon sen 138
Thailand-Modern
Chilli mussels with rice noodles 140
Glass noodle som tum 141
Thai chicken noodle soup 142
Beef and glass noodle salad 143

Mee krob

It doesn't matter how many times I make this dish, I'm like a child gazing in wonder when the noodles puff up in the oil. In Thailand, the ingredients for mee krob vary according to what's in season and what's on hand, so feel free to improvise a little. This is a big favourite at parties.

peanut oil, for deep frying
125 g (4 oz) rice vermicelli
4 cloves of garlic, finely chopped
6 shallots, finely chopped
150 g (5 oz) pork loin, finely chopped
150 g (5 oz) chicken breast, finely chopped
150 g (5 oz) prawn meat, finely chopped
1 small red chilli, finely sliced
120 g (4 oz) hard bean curd, diced
2 tbsp palm sugar
2 tbsp fish sauce (nam pla)
2 tbsp vinegar
juice of 1 lime
100 g (3 oz) bean sprouts

To serve
2 fresh red chillies, sliced
½ cup coriander leaves
3 spring onions, finely chopped

Heat oil in a hot wok or deep fryer until almost smoking. Cut noodles into manageable lengths with a pair of scissors, and deep fry a handful at a time. When noodles puff up and turn golden (a matter of seconds) remove.

Pour off oil, leaving 1 tablespoon. Fry garlic and shallot until they start to colour. Add pork, chicken, prawns, chilli and bean curd and lightly stir fry for 3 minutes. Add sugar, fish sauce and vinegar and cook, stirring, for 30 seconds.

Add lime juice, bean sprouts and noodles and toss quickly, then immediately bring to the table before mixture softens. Scatter with chilli, coriander leaves and spring onion. Serve with forks and spoons.

For a more dramatic effect, put crisp noodles on a large serving plate. Pour on the sauce, and scatter with chilli, bean sprouts, coriander leaves and spring onion. Top with more crisp noodles. Bring to the table and serve.

Serves four.

Gwaytio neua sap

Thai people are particularly fond of fresh rice noodles and incorporate them into a number of truly original dishes. Yet for some strange reason, very few of these dishes ever seem to make it out of Thailand. Unusually gentle in its spicing, this homely noodle dish lets the textures do the talking, playing off the soft silky feel of the noodle against the crisp crunch of lettuce leaves and bean sprouts.

500 g (1 lb) fresh rice sheet noodles, cut into 1 cm (½ in) strips
4 tbsp peanut oil
3 shallots, finely chopped
2 cloves of garlic, finely chopped
200 g (7 oz) finely minced beef
100 g (3 oz) bean sprouts, blanched briefly
    in boiling water and rinsed in cold
1 tbsp light soy sauce
1 tbsp fish sauce (nam pla)
200 ml (7 fl oz) chicken stock
1 tbsp preserved shredded Thai radish
1 tsp cornflour, mixed with a little water
1 tbsp dark soy sauce
6 lettuce leaves, roughly torn
1 spring onion, finely sliced
1 small bunch of coriander leaves, roughly chopped

Pour boiling water over noodles in a heatproof bowl and carefully separate noodles with chopsticks. Drain as quickly as possible.

Heat 2 tablespoons of oil in a hot wok and brown shallot, adding garlic towards the end of browning time. Add beef and cook over high heat until it changes colour. Reduce heat and add bean sprouts, light soy sauce, fish sauce, stock and preserved radish. When sauce begins to boil, add cornflour mixture and stir well until thickened. Transfer to a saucepan and keep warm.

Heat remaining oil in a hot wok and stir fry noodles with dark soy sauce for 1 minute. Arrange lettuce on a serving plate and tip noodles out onto the bed of lettuce.

Pour sauce over noodles. Scatter with spring onion and coriander leaves, and serve with forks and spoons.

Serves four.

Kao soi

Also known as Chiang Mai noodles, this northern Thai dish of curried noodles with its crackling topping of crisp, deep-fried noodles has been called the Thai answer to Malaysian laksa. But *kao soi*, which shows heavy Burmese influences, has a complexity and character all its own.

vegetable oil, for deep frying
400 g (14 oz) fresh egg noodles
3 chicken marylands (leg and thigh)
2½ cups coconut milk
2 tbsp Thai red curry paste (see Basics, page 191)
½ tsp ground turmeric
½ tsp ground cumin
1 tbsp fish sauce (nam pla)
1 tsp sugar
1 tsp salt
2½ cups chicken stock
2 spring onions, green part only, finely sliced
3 tbsp coriander, roughly chopped
2 limes, halved

To serve
4 shallots, thinly sliced
1 tbsp crushed dried chilli
½ cup Thai pickled mustard cabbage

Heat oil in a hot wok and deep fry a quarter of the noodles until crisp and golden, about 1 minute. Drain on paper towels. Cook remaining noodles in boiling water for a minute. Rinse with cold water, drain and set aside.

Chop chicken marylands across the bone into 2 cm (¾ in) pieces. In a clean wok, heat 1 cup of the thicker coconut milk that has risen to the surface, and fry red curry paste, turmeric and cumin until the fragrant aroma tells you it's ready – about 2 to 3 minutes. Add chicken and stir fry for 2 minutes. Add remaining coconut milk, fish sauce, sugar, salt and stock and simmer, stirring, for 15 minutes.

Rinse noodles in boiling water to heat. Drain and divide among 4 large soup bowls. Ladle soup and chicken into bowls and top with fried noodles, spring onion and coriander. Place half a lime in each bowl and serve with shallots, dried chilli and pickled mustard cabbage. Serve with forks and spoons.

Serves four.

Thailand   *Noodle i-d **2***

Khanom jeen with spicy pork

Yet another Oriental alternative to good old spag bol, and this time it even comes with tomato. The soft, bland nature of the rice noodles is the perfect foil for the intensely spicy sauce, proving that opposites not only attract, they can get on like a house on fire.

1 tbsp vegetable oil
2 tbsp Thai red curry paste (see Basics, page 191)
1 tsp ground turmeric
750 g (1½ lb) minced pork
3 tomatoes, cut into wedges
1 tbsp yellow bean sauce (taucheo), mashed
2 tbsp fish sauce (nam pla)
1 tbsp lime juice
500 g (1 lb) fresh round rice noodles (khanom jeen), or thin bun noodles
4 tbsp crisp garlic flakes (available from Asian grocery stores)
1½ cups coriander leaves
2 spring onions, green part only, finely sliced
1½ cups bean sprouts
1 lime, cut into wedges

Heat oil in a hot wok and fry curry paste and turmeric for 1 minute. Add minced pork and stir well. Reduce heat and gently stir fry for 4 to 5 minutes. Add tomato and cook for 3 to 4 minutes. Add bean sauce, fish sauce and lime juice. Cover and keep warm.

Pour boiling water over noodles and separate them gently with a chopstick. Drain well, and arrange on a large serving platter. Pour sauce over the noodles and mix well. Scatter with garlic flakes, coriander leaves and spring onion and serve with bean sprouts and lime wedges on the side. Serve with forks and spoons.

Serves four.

Moo sarong

I was first taught this recipe by the very urbane Chalie Amatyakul, who started the esteemed Hotel Oriental Thai Cooking School in Bangkok. Looking like miniature balls of knitting yarn, these wrapped meatballs can be a lot of fun to make, as long as you realise that you don't have to be absolutely perfect with your wrapping.

500 g (1 lb) lean pork
4 water chestnuts
4 dried shiitake mushrooms, soaked for 30 minutes
3 shallots
3 cloves of garlic
4 coriander roots
2 tbsp fresh coriander leaves, chopped
6 white peppercorns
½ tsp salt
1 small egg, lightly beaten
1 tbsp cornflour
200 g (7 oz) rice vermicelli
peanut oil, for deep frying
4 tbsp sweet chilli sauce

Finely chop pork, water chestnuts, mushrooms and shallots to a fine mince. Chop garlic, coriander roots and leaves and grind or pound with peppercorns and salt in a mortar and pestle until smooth.

Put spice paste and pork mixture in a bowl, add beaten egg and cornflour, and use your hands to combine thoroughly. Form into small balls, about 2.5 cm (1 in) in diameter.

Cover noodles with boiling water and leave for about 6 or 7 minutes, until soft. Drain well. Toss with a little oil to prevent sticking.

Take 1 strand and carefully wrap it around a meatball, turning the meatball slightly in your hand as you do, so that the noodles line up side by side. Keep going, as if it is a ball of twine, until there is no meat visible, only noodle. Don't worry if it looks loose or untidy – it doesn't really matter.

Heat oil in a large hot wok and deep fry wrapped meatballs until golden and crisp. Serve with sweet chilli sauce, for dipping.

Serves 8 as an appetiser.

Thailand   *Noodle i-d 8*   135

Pad Thai

When people refer to 'Thai noodles', they usually mean pad Thai. Jumping with flavour and dead easy to make, this is a dish that's equally at home at a dinner party, in a street hawker's wok, or on the finest china of an upmarket restaurant.

180 g (6 oz) rice stick noodles
2 tbsp dried shrimp
4 tbsp peanut oil
2 shallots, chopped
2 cloves of garlic, finely chopped
2 eggs, beaten
2 tbsp fish sauce (nam pla)
1 tbsp lime juice
1 tsp sugar
1 tbsp tomato ketchup
2 tbsp roasted chopped peanuts
1 cup bean sprouts
1 dried chilli, ground
1 tbsp shredded Thai preserved radish
2 spring onions, cut into 2.5 cm (1 in) pieces
200 g (7 oz) small prawns, cooked
2 tbsp chopped coriander
1 lime, cut into wedges

Soak noodles in hot water for about 15 minutes, or until soft. Rinse in cold water, and drain.

Place dried shrimp in a coffee grinder reserved for spices and grind to a powder.

Heat oil in a hot wok and cook shallot for a few minutes until golden. Add garlic and cook for 1 minute, taking care not to let it burn. Add beaten egg, allow it to set for a minute or two, then stir with a spoon. Add drained noodles, tossing well to combine with the egg. Add fish sauce, lime juice, sugar, ketchup, half each of the peanuts, shrimp powder and bean sprouts, the chilli, preserved radish, spring onion and prawns. Stir constantly until heated through.

Transfer to a serving dish and sprinkle with remaining shrimp powder, peanuts, bean sprouts and the coriander. Add a lime wedge or 2 to each plate. Serve with forks and spoons.

Serves four.

Seafood and glass noodle salad

The real secret of this wonderfully refreshing summer salad is the dried shrimp powder, which imbues the whole thing with what I can only describe as an enchanting Thai accent. It's a good idea to keep a small electric coffee grinder just for grinding your spices, but never use the one you use for your coffee beans. A quick whiz, and you have instant shrimp powder.

150 g (5 oz) bean thread vermicelli
150 g (5 oz) squid tubes, cleaned
1 tbsp peanut oil
150 g (5 oz) small green prawns, peeled and deveined
2 cloves of garlic, finely chopped
2 tbsp peanuts, roughly chopped
2 tbsp fish sauce (nam pla)
2 spring onions, green part only, sliced
2 tbsp coriander, chopped
2 tbsp lime juice
2 red chillies, chopped
2 tbsp dried shrimp powder (see page 136)

Pour boiling water over noodles and leave to stand for 3 to 5 minutes. Drain and rinse under cold water. Drain again.

Cut squid into pieces roughly 2.5 cm (1 in) square, and score the underside in a criss-cross pattern with the tip of a sharp knife.

Heat oil in a hot wok and quickly stir fry squid and prawns until prawns just change colour, a little more than 1 minute.

Combine noodles and seafood in a bowl with the garlic, peanuts, fish sauce, spring onion, coriander, lime juice, chilli and shrimp powder. Serve warm or at room temperature with forks and spoons.

Serves four.

Pad woon sen

Always a dramatic dish to make because of the appealing see-through nature of the cellophane noodles, this quick and easy stir fry is a popular lunchtime snack throughout Thailand. If the noodles start getting hard to handle, a few snips here and there with a pair of scissors will cut them down to size.

200 g (7 oz) bean thread vermicelli
3 tbsp vegetable oil
3 cloves of garlic, finely chopped
100 g (3 oz) lean pork, finely sliced
150 g (5 oz) small prawns, peeled
2 tbsp fish sauce (nam pla)
2 stalks of celery with leaves, finely chopped
2 tbsp light soy sauce
2 tbsp chicken stock
100 g (3 oz) bean sprouts, lightly blanched
1 tsp sugar
ground white pepper, to taste
2 tbsp coriander leaves
4 tbsp roasted peanuts, coarsely crushed
1 lime, quartered

Pour boiling water over noodles and soak for 3 to 5 minutes. Drain.

Heat oil in a hot wok and fry garlic until golden. Add pork and stir fry until meat is opaque. Add prawns and stir fry for 1 minute. Add noodles and toss lightly.

Add fish sauce, celery, soy sauce, chicken stock, bean sprouts, sugar and white pepper. Heat through and serve on a large platter or in small Asian bowls. Scatter with coriander and peanuts and serve with a quartered lime. Serve with forks and spoons.

Serves four.

Thailand   *Noodle i-d 11*

Chilli mussels with rice noodles

Mussels, clams and pippis take on a luscious, seductive character when powered by the dense fiery tang of chilli paste. Traditionally, this dish would be served with rice, but rice noodles are equally compatible. Fresh rice ribbon noodles would work just as well.

1.5 kg (3 lb) mussels
3 tbsp peanut oil
3 cloves of garlic, chopped
3 red chillies, finely chopped
1 tbsp freshly grated ginger
½ cup dry white wine
400 g (14 oz) fresh round rice noodles (khanom jeen),
   or thin Vietnamese bun noodles
2 tbsp fish sauce (nam pla)
1 tbsp chilli paste (jam) or sweet chilli sauce
1 tbsp lime juice
small bunch of coriander
1 lime, quartered

Leave mussels in a pot of cold water, changing the water two or three times, for about 4 hours. Remove beards from mussels and lightly scrub the shells.

In a heavy-bottomed pan, heat oil and stir fry garlic, chilli and ginger for 1 minute. Add white wine and turn up the heat. Add mussels and cook, covered, for 1 to 2 minutes on high heat. Remove lid and take out any mussels that have opened. Cover for another 30 seconds, remove lid and use kitchen tongs to take out any more mussels that have opened. Continue this process another two or three times. Discard any that do not open.

Place noodles in a heatproof bowl and cover with boiling water.

Gently separate noodles with a chopstick, taking care not to break or damage them. Drain well, arrange noodles on a large serving platter and put mussels on top.

Add fish sauce, chilli jam and lime juice to the cooking juices and bring to the boil, stirring. Taste and adjust flavours accordingly. Pour over mussels and noodles, scatter with roughly chopped coriander leaves and quartered lime, and serve.

Serves four.

Glass noodle som tum

With its delectable crunch and sassy sweet-and-sour flavours, there is absolutely nothing wrong with the traditional som tum green papaya salad just as it is. But when I see a perfect noodle opportunity just waiting to be snapped up, I can't help myself.

200 g (7 oz) bean thread vermicelli
½ green (unripe) papaya
6 green beans
2 ripe tomatoes
4 shallots, peeled and very thinly sliced
1 clove of garlic, crushed with the side of a knife blade
1 red chilli
1 tbsp dried shrimp
1 tbsp palm sugar
3 tbsp mint leaves
2 tbsp lime juice
2 tbsp fish sauce (nam pla)
2 tbsp roasted peanuts, crushed

Soak noodles in boiling water for 3 to 5 minutes. Rinse in cold water, drain well and set aside.

Peel papaya and remove seeds. Slice flesh finely, then cut each slice into thin matchsticks. Drain, rinse in cold water and set aside. Cut beans into fine matchsticks and cook in simmering, salted water for 30 seconds. Drain, rinse under cold water and set aside. Cut the thick outer flesh from tomatoes and discard the rest. Slice tomato into slivers.

In a mortar or heavy bowl, pound the shallot, garlic and chilli until mushy. Add shrimp and palm sugar and continue to pound to a rough paste. Add beans, tomato and mint leaves and toss. Add lime juice and fish sauce to taste. Add papaya and noodles and toss lightly. Pile high on a serving platter and scatter with crushed peanuts.

Serves 4 as a salad.

Thai chicken noodle soup

Tom kha gai, creamy, coconutty, galangal-powered chicken soup, is second only to the great *tom yam goong* in Thailand's top-of-the-pops soups. By adding rice noodles, you get an effect not unlike a Thai curry laksa.

2 stalks of lemongrass, white part only
400 g (14 oz) chicken meat
1 cup chicken stock
4 cups coconut milk
4 kaffir lime leaves
5 slices galangal
½ tsp salt
1 tsp sugar
2 tbsp fish sauce (nam pla)
2 small red chillies, sliced
2 tbsp lime juice
300 g (10 oz) fresh round rice noodles (khanom jeen),
    or 300 g (10 oz) cooked rice vermicelli
3 tbsp coriander leaves

Bruise lemongrass and cut into 2.5 cm (1 in) pieces. Cut chicken meat into bite-size pieces. Bring chicken stock and half the coconut milk to the boil, and add chicken, lemongrass, lime leaves, galangal, salt, sugar, and 1 tbsp fish sauce. Simmer for 15 minutes.

Stir in remaining coconut milk. Toss in chillies and add remaining fish sauce and lime juice to taste. Remove from the heat.

Put noodles in a heatproof bowl and cover with boiling water. Separate gently with chopsticks, then drain well and distribute among 4 deep soup bowls. Ladle soup and chicken over the noodles and sprinkle coriander leaves over the top. Serve with forks and spoons.

Serves four.

Beef and glass noodle salad

Another Thai classic (*yam neua* or rare-beef salad) gets the noodle treatment and is transformed into something thoroughly wonderful. The glossy, slippery noodles not only add texture and interest, but also tend to lighten the dish, taking a little of the heaviness away from the meat.

250 g (8 oz) bean thread vermicelli
1 tbsp jasmine rice
3 dried chillies
400 g (14 oz) fillet steak
6 shallots, finely sliced
3 spring onions, finely sliced
3 tbsp lime juice
3 tbsp fish sauce (nam pla)
1 tsp sugar
1 cup fresh mint leaves
1 cup Asian basil or coriander

Pour boiling water over noodles in a heatproof bowl and let stand for 3 to 5 minutes. Rinse in cold water and drain well. With a pair of scissors, roughly cut the noodles so they are a manageable length, and set aside.

Toast rice in a dry, heavy-bottomed frying pan until lightly golden. Grind or pound rice to a powder and set aside.

Toast dried chillies until quite smoky, then grind to a powder and set aside.

Grill steak quickly so it is still quite rare, and leave to rest for about 15 minutes.

Mix 1 teaspoon of the freshly roasted chilli powder with rice powder, shallot, spring onion, lime juice, fish sauce and sugar in a large bowl. Slice beef thinly and add it to the mixture, along with the noodles, mint, Asian basil or coriander. Toss lightly and serve piled high on a large platter.

Serves four.

Vietnam

Bun rieu noodle soup with
crab dumplings 146
Bun bo Hué 148
Cellophane noodles with prawns 149
Cha gio (finger-size spring rolls) 150
Goi cuon (fresh spring rolls) 151
Pho bo 152
Pho ga 153
Nem nuong 154

Bun rieu noodle soup with crab dumplings

This intriguingly aromatic noodle and crab dumpling soup is usually made with the small, freshwater crabs found in rice paddies. If you don't happen to have a rice paddy nearby, any crab will do, as long as it's fresh.

120 g (4 oz) minced pork
3 tbsp dried shrimp, soaked for 30 minutes and drained
200 g (7 oz) crab meat, cooked
1 tsp shrimp paste
pinch of salt
pinch of pepper
1 small egg, lightly beaten
2 tbsp peanut oil
4 shallots, finely sliced
2 cloves of garlic, finely chopped
2 red chillies, sliced
3 tomatoes, cut into wedges
2 litres (3½ pts) chicken stock
2 tbsp fish sauce (nuoc mam)
½ tsp sugar
1 tbsp white rice vinegar
400 g (14 oz) thin fresh round rice noodles (bun)
1 cup bean sprouts
2 spring onions, finely sliced
1 bunch ngo gai (saw-leaf plant), or coriander
2 limes, cut into wedges
leaves from 1 small bunch mint

Using a food processor, or mortar and pestle, combine pork, drained shrimp and half the crab meat until it forms a smooth paste. Transfer to a bowl and mix in shrimp paste, salt, pepper and remaining crab by hand. Beat in egg with a fork and refrigerate for an hour.

Heat oil in a saucepan and cook shallot for 2 to 3 minutes. Add garlic and half the red chilli and cook for another 30 seconds. Add tomato and cook for 1 minute. Add stock, fish sauce, sugar and vinegar. Bring soup to a simmer.

Mould 1 tablespoon of dumpling mixture into a football shape and gently add it to the boiling stock. Repeat until all the dumpling mixture is used. Cover and simmer for 4 minutes, or until dumplings are firm and floating.

Pour boiling water over noodles in a heatproof bowl. Gently shake loose with a chopstick, drain, and divide among 4 soup bowls. Top with bean sprouts, spring onion, dumplings and soup. Serve with a bowl of ngo gai or coriander leaves, lime wedges, mint leaves and remaining chopped chilli to be added according to individual taste.

Serves four.

Bun bo Hué

This hearty, dense, satisfying soup comes from the city of Hué in central Vietnam, the one-time capital of French Indochina and the home of imperial cooking. A city known for its ritual tea drinking and elaborate, time-consuming dishes, it still manages to find room for a little comfort food every now and then.

2.5 litres (4 pts) beef stock
1 stalk of lemongrass, bruised
300 g (10 oz) boned leg pork or pork shank
2 tbsp peanut oil
200 g (7 oz) sirloin, rump or fillet steak, finely sliced
6 shallots or 1 onion, finely sliced
1 stalk of lemongrass, white heart only, finely sliced
2 red chillies, finely sliced
½ tsp sugar
pinch of salt
¼ cup coriander leaves
1 tbsp fish sauce (nuoc mam)
400 g (14 oz) fresh round rice noodles (bun)
1 spring onion, finely sliced
1 cup loosely packed bean sprouts
¼ cup mint leaves or Asian basil leaves

Put beef stock, bruised lemongrass and pork in a saucepan and bring to the boil. Skim off any froth that rises to the surface, reduce heat and simmer for 30 minutes. Remove pork and slice thinly.

Heat 1 tablespoon oil in a hot wok and briefly stir fry beef slices for about 1 minute. Reserve. Heat remaining oil in a hot wok and cook shallot until soft and golden. Add sliced lemongrass and half the chilli, stir fry for a minute or two, then add mixture to stock along with sugar, salt, coriander and fish sauce, and simmer for a minute.

Pour boiling water over fresh noodles and separate them gently with chopsticks. Drain and divide noodles among 4 large soup bowls. Top with a few beef slices, some pork, spring onion and the hot soup. Serve with bean sprouts, mint leaves and remaining chilli.

Serves four.

Cellophane noodles with prawns

Traditionally, these noodles are cooked with crab meat and served as an appetiser. However, the dish takes on more structure when prawns are substituted and, to my mind, works equally well either as a starter or served as part of a main meal with other dishes.

15 g (½ oz) dried black fungus
150 g (5 oz) bean thread vermicelli
2 tbsp peanut oil
1 onion, sliced thinly
3 cloves of garlic, finely chopped
300 g (10 oz) green prawns, peeled
150 ml (¼ pt) chicken stock
2 tbsp fish sauce (nuoc mam)
2 tbsp lime juice
½ tsp salt
1 tsp sugar
2 spring onions, green part only, thinly sliced
2 tbsp chopped coriander

Cover fungus with boiling water in a bowl and leave to stand for 1 hour. Chop roughly.

Pour boiling water over noodles and soak for 3 to 4 minutes. Drain and cut into roughly 15 cm (6 in) lengths.

Heat oil in a hot wok and fry onion for a few minutes until it starts to brown. Add garlic and cook for another 30 seconds.

Add prawns and fungus and stir through just until prawns start to change colour. Add noodles and stir fry for 1 minute. Add stock, fish sauce, lime juice, salt and sugar and cook until most of the liquid has disappeared. Scatter with spring onion and coriander and serve.

Serves four.

Cha gio (finger-size spring rolls)

What makes this dish special is the way it is eaten. The crisp, deep-fried rolls are wrapped with fresh herbs and lettuce leaves, then dipped in sweet/sour/spicy nuoc cham sauce. Textures and flavours dash about the mouth like excited schoolchildren.

50 g (2 oz) bean thread vermicelli
200 g (7 oz) chicken mince
200 g (7 oz) pork mince
100 g (3 oz) canned or fresh crab meat
100 g (3 oz) green prawns, peeled and finely chopped
2 tbsp dried wood ear fungus, soaked for 1 hour and shredded
2 cloves of garlic, finely chopped
4 shallots, finely chopped
1 tbsp fish sauce (nuoc mam)
½ tsp white pepper
4 cups warm water
1 tbsp white vinegar
1 tbsp sugar
30 small rounds rice paper (banh trang)
1 tbsp cornflour mixed with 1 tbsp cold water
peanut oil, for deep frying
leaves from iceberg lettuce, roughly torn
1 bunch Asian basil or common mint
1 bunch Vietnamese mint (rau ram)
1 quantity nuoc cham (see Basics, page 192)

Soak noodles in boiling water for 3 to 4 minutes, rinse in cold water, drain and cut into roughly 6 cm (2½ in) lengths.

In a bowl, combine meats, crab, prawn, fungus, noodles, garlic, shallot, fish sauce and pepper.

Combine warm water with vinegar and sugar in a bowl and soak each rice paper until soft and pliable. Drain on a dry tea-towel and repeat the process.

Take a softened paper and put a tablespoon of filling just above the centre. Bring the top edge of the paper down over the filling and roll it over itself once. Tuck in both ends and continue rolling tightly until it resembles a thin cigar about 7.5 cm (3 in) long. Moisten the bottom of the rice paper with a little cornflour paste and press to seal.

Heat oil in wok until a cube of bread dances on the surface. Cook the rolls, a few at a time, for about 5 minutes, or until lightly golden and cooked through.

To eat, wrap each roll in a lettuce leaf, tucking in Asian basil and Vietnamese mint along the way. Serve with nuoc cham sauce for dipping.

Serves four.

Goi cuon (fresh spring rolls)

In England, America and Australia, fresh spring rolls are currently riding the crest of the fusion popularity wave. Inventive young chefs all over the world are stuffing them with all manner of weird and not-always-wonderful things. The real secret, however, is to keep the filling fresh and relatively simple. The other secret is to eat them as soon as they are made.

100 g (3 oz) rice vermicelli
8 rounds dried rice paper (banh trang)
1 cup shredded iceberg lettuce
4 tbsp fresh bean sprouts
4 tbsp beer nuts
bunch of fresh mint, picked
bunch of fresh coriander, picked
16 flat garlic chives
16 small prawns, cooked and peeled
1 quantity nuoc cham (see Basics, page 192)

Pour boiling water over noodles in a heatproof bowl and leave for 6 to 7 minutes. Drain, then transfer to a saucepan of boiling water and cook for one more minute. Rinse in cold water and drain again.

Dunk each rice paper round in boiling water for a few seconds until soft. Spread out to drain on serving plates.

On each paper put some shredded lettuce, noodles, bean sprouts, beer nuts, mint and coriander, and fold the rice paper towards the centre to form a firm roll. Tuck in 2 small prawns, fold in ends of rice paper and place 2 garlic chives in the crease so they protrude by about 2.5 cm (1 in). Roll into a neat sausage shape. The rice paper will stick to itself and hold the shape. Serve with nuoc cham dipping sauce.

Makes eight.

Pho bo

What began life as an honest labourer's breakfast dish of noodle soup laced with beefy bits has gone on to hijack lunchtimes all over the world.

1 kg (2 lb) beef bones
4 litres (7 pts) water
2 onions, quartered
1 tsp salt
2 knobs of ginger, about 2.5 cm (1 in) round
5 cardamom pods
3 pieces star anise
1 cinnamon stick
500 g (1 lb) beef brisket
2 tbsp fish sauce (nuoc mam)
500 g (1 lb) fresh rice sheet noodles
250 g (8 oz) fillet steak, sliced paper-thin
1 onion, very finely sliced
4 spring onions, finely chopped
white pepper

Accompaniments
extra fish sauce (nuoc mam)
hoisin sauce (optional)
2 limes, cut into wedges
3 small fresh chillies, chopped
sprig each of Asian basil, coriander and Vietnamese mint
2 cups bean sprouts, washed

Put bones in a large saucepan with the water, 1 quartered onion, salt, 1 knob of ginger, cardamom pods, star anise and cinnamon. Grill remaining quartered onion and ginger until skins are burnt, add them to the stock and bring to the boil. Skim off any froth that rises, add the brisket, bring to the boil and skim again. Add fish sauce and simmer for 4 hours.

Remove brisket and slice half of it very finely. Strain stock into a jug or saucepan.

Cut rice noodles into 1 cm (½ in) strips, and put in a large heatproof bowl. Cover with boiling water for 20 seconds, gently separating noodles with chopsticks. Drain and divide noodles among 6 bowls. Top with 3 or 4 slices of brisket and raw steak. Then add a few onion slices and some spring onion.

Bring soup to the boil, ladle over meat and noodles and sprinkle with pepper. Flavour with extra fish sauce or hoisin sauce to taste. Add any or all of the accompaniments as you wish.

Serves six.

Pho ga

The real, the true, the original *pho* (pronounced somewhere between far and fer) is *pho bo*. Yet this chicken version is every bit as satisfying and complex, albeit lighter, sweeter and a touch more subtle.

3 litres (5 pts) water
1 tsp salt
1 whole chicken, about 1.5 kg (3 lb), preferably with head and feet
1 kg (2 lb) chicken bones
2 white onions, finely sliced
5 cm (2 in) knob of fresh ginger, peeled and sliced
1 cinnamon stick
1 star anise
3 cardamom pods
2 tsp white sugar
4 tbsp deep-fried shallots (available from Asian grocery stores)
3 tbsp fish sauce (nuoc mam)
400 g (14 oz) fresh rice sheet noodles
4 spring onions, finely sliced
8 coriander sprigs

Accompaniments
1 cup bean sprouts
sprigs of fresh mint
sprigs of Asian basil
sprigs of coriander
1 red chilli, finely chopped
1 lemon or lime, cut into wedges

Combine water, salt, whole chicken, chicken bones, 1 sliced onion, ginger, cinnamon, star anise and cardamom pods in a large pot and bring to the boil. Skim off any froth that rises to the surface, lower heat and simmer for 1½ hours. Remove whole chicken and reserve.

Add sugar, 2 tablespoons deep-fried shallots and fish sauce to stock and cook for another hour. Strain stock through a fine sieve. Slice chicken thigh and breast finely.

Cut rice noodles (if not pre-cut) into 1 cm (½ in) strips, like tagliatelle. Put in a heatproof bowl, cover with boiling water, shake gently apart with chopsticks and drain.

To assemble soup, divide rice noodles among 4 deep soup bowls. Layer chicken meat neatly on top and spoon hot soup into each bowl. Scatter remaining deep-fried shallots, spring onion and coriander on top.

Serve with an accompanying platter of bean sprouts, herbs, chilli and lemon or lime wedges for each person to add according to their taste.

Serves four.

Nem nuong

The Vietnamese have a happy knack of turning practically any grilled meat into a complete meal just by serving it on a bed of rice noodles and accompanying it with a bowl of nuoc cham. Rarely, however, does the idea work as well as it does with these moist, delicious pork meatballs served on a bed of rice vermicelli.

1 tbsp jasmine rice
500 g (1 lb) boned pork shoulder or neck
2 tbsp sugar
2 tbsp fish sauce (nuoc mam)
3 cloves of garlic, finely chopped
¼ tsp white pepper
100 g (3 oz) pork fat, chopped into small cubes
1 tsp salt
pinch of baking powder
250 g (8 oz) rice vermicelli
1 cup loosely packed bean sprouts
1 small cucumber, peeled and sliced
½ cup peanuts, roughly chopped
small bunch Asian basil, or fresh mint, picked
1 quantity nuoc cham (see Basics, page 192)

Toast rice in a dry, heavy-bottomed frying pan until lightly golden. Grind or pound rice to a coarse powder and set aside. Soak 8 wooden skewers in cold water for 1 hour to stop them from burning on the grill.

Cut pork into thin strips and mix with sugar, fish sauce, garlic and pepper. Cover and let stand for 30 minutes.

Transfer meat to a food processor with pork fat, ground roasted rice and salt and whiz until it is a pale, smooth paste. Mix in baking powder with your hands and, using hands again, roll mixture into balls the size of small plums. Thread balls onto wooden skewers and char-grill until nice and brown.

Meanwhile, cover noodles in boiling water and leave for 6 to 7 minutes. Drain, then transfer to a saucepan of boiling water and cook for one more minute. Rinse in cold water and drain. Put a little vermicelli on each plate and top with the meatballs. On a separate plate, arrange bean sprouts, cucumber, peanuts and herbs. The meatballs can also be wrapped in rice paper rounds and lettuce leaves at the table. Serve with nuoc cham for dipping.

Serves four.

Korea

Chap chae

Normal Chinese bean thread noodles will work well in this much-loved noodle, beef and vegetable stir fry, but it's worth sniffing out a Korean food store for genuine dang myun. The extra body and extra chew in these Korean potato starch noodles gives the dish much more body and presence.

200 g (7 oz) dang myun or bean thread vermicelli
400 g (14 oz) good quality beef fillet, cut into thick matchstick strips
2 tsp sugar
4 tbsp dark soy sauce
4 cloves of garlic, finely chopped
2 spring onions, finely sliced
2 tsp sesame oil
1 tbsp sesame seeds, lightly roasted in a dry pan
2 dried shiitake mushrooms
5 tbsp peanut oil
2 eggs, beaten
½ carrot, cut into matchsticks
1 medium onion, sliced into thin matchsticks
1 cup loosely packed bean sprouts, washed
¼ Peking cabbage, shredded
1 small cucumber, cut into matchsticks
½ cup fresh wood ear fungus,
    or 4 abalone or oyster mushrooms, cut into strips
salt, to taste
pinch of ground dried chilli
1 tbsp pinenuts

Boil noodles in plenty of water for 3 minutes. Rinse in cold water, drain and cut into 12 cm (5 in) lengths. Combine beef, 1 teaspoon sugar, 2 tablespoons soy sauce, garlic, spring onion, 1 teaspoon sesame oil and the sesame seeds, and marinate for an hour.

Soak shiitake mushrooms in hot water for 1 hour. Drain, discard stems and cut caps into fine strips. Using 1 tablespoon of oil and the beaten eggs, make omelette according to directions on page 190.

Heat 2 tablespoons oil in a hot wok and cook carrot and onion until they soften. Add bean sprouts and cabbage and stir fry for 2 minutes. Stir cucumber through mixture and set aside.

Heat remaining 2 tablespoons oil in a hot wok and stir fry beef, fungus and mushrooms for 2 minutes. Add noodles, remaining 2 tablespoons soy sauce, 1 teaspoon each sugar and sesame oil, a pinch of salt and chilli. Stir in vegetables and pinenuts, and heat through, stirring, for 3 minutes. Serve on a large platter, topped with omelette strips. Serve with chopsticks.

Serves four.

Korea   *Noodle i-d* **19**

Bibim naeng myun

Crisp is not a word that usually springs to mind when you talk about boiled noodles, but this Korean favourite is lifted considerably by a veritable chorus line of in-your-face crunches. The addition of cucumber, daikon and nashi pear also gives the dish a curiously pleasing flavour twist.

300 g (10 oz) naeng myun
2 tbsp sesame oil
2 cloves of garlic, finely chopped
2 tbsp gochu jang chilli paste
4 tbsp Korean beef broth (see Basics, page 193)
2 tbsp soy sauce
2 tbsp sugar
1 tsp sesame seeds
1 small cucumber
½ tsp salt
1 nashi pear
100 g (3 oz) Korean daikon pickles (see Basics, page 193)
16 slices cooked beef (from beef broth, above)
2 spring onions, green part only, finely sliced
2 hard-boiled eggs, halved

Cook noodles in boiling water for 4 to 5 minutes. Rinse under cold water and drain. Toss through 1 tablespoon sesame oil, cover and refrigerate.

To make sauce, mix garlic, chilli paste, remaining sesame oil, beef stock, soy sauce, sugar and sesame seeds together. Peel cucumber in half lengthwise and discard seeds. Cut into thin slices, sprinkle with salt and leave for 10 minutes. Drain and dry with paper towels. Peel pear and cut into matchsticks about 6 cm (2½ in) long.

Divide noodles among 4 large soup bowls. Arrange a little of the cucumber, pear, daikon pickle, 4 slices of beef, some spring onion and half a hard-boiled egg on top of the noodles.

Divide sauce among 4 small bowls and give one to each person to use as little or as much as desired. The sauce is added to the noodles, then the whole thing is tossed before eating. Serve at room temperature with chopsticks.

Serves four.

Kalgooksu

Koreans have a happy knack of being able to get beef into practically every dish they cook. This combination of beef strips with a highly flavoured anchovy stock may seem odd at first, but the end result is surprisingly soothing and even tastes vaguely familiar.

500 g (1 lb) clams
250 g (8 oz) sirloin or rump steak
3 tbsp soy sauce
2 red chillies, thinly sliced
1 tbsp sesame oil
2 tbsp toasted sesame seeds
¼ tsp black pepper
3 cloves of garlic, crushed with the side of a knife blade
3 spring onions, finely sliced, keeping green and white parts separate
½ tsp ground cayenne pepper
2 litres (3½ pts) water
20 dried anchovies (from Korean or Japanese grocery stores)
1 small carrot, cut into thin matchsticks
400 g (14 oz) dried round gooksu white wheat noodles
2 small zucchinis, cut into matchsticks
¼ cup white wine
1 tbsp peanut oil

Leave clams in a pot of cold water, changing the water two or three times, for about 4 hours.

Cut beef into strips 2.5 cm (1 in) long and 1 cm (½ in) thick. Combine with 2 tablespoons soy sauce, chilli, sesame oil and seeds, pepper, garlic, half the spring onion greens and the cayenne. Cover and let stand for 20 minutes.

Bring water to the boil. Add anchovies and simmer for 10 minutes. Strain and discard anchovies. Add 1 tablespoon soy sauce, carrot, white parts of spring onion and noodles and simmer for 4 minutes. Add zucchini and cook for a further 3 minutes.

Meanwhile, put clams and white wine in a saucepan, cover and steam until clams open. Remove clams, strain broth through muslin and reserve. If the clam stock is not too salty, add it to the anchovy stock.

Heat peanut oil in a hot wok, add beef mixture and stir fry for 2 minutes. Divide noodles among 4 serving bowls and pour stock and vegetables over the top. In neat little clumps on top, add a few clams, a little nest of beef strips and a pile of the remaining spring onion greens. Serve with chopsticks and spoons.

Serves four.

Mandu kuk

Mandu are beef dumplings that bear more than a passing resemblance to Japanese gyoza or the Chinese wor tip. They can be pan fried or deep fried, but are at their best when boiled and served in soup. If you don't feel like making them yourself, you can buy ready-made frozen dumplings from Korean and Japanese grocery stores. The addition of dang myun noodles turns the whole thing into a kind of won ton noodle soup with attitude.

100 g (3 oz) dang myun
2 litres (3½ pts) Korean beef broth (see Basics, page 193)
250 g (8 oz) minced beef
1 small onion, finely chopped
4 cloves of garlic, finely chopped
3 tbsp soy sauce
1 tbsp sesame oil
2 cups bean sprouts, blanched
12 Mandu dumplings (see Basics, page 192), cooked
3 spring onions, green part only, finely sliced

Put noodles in boiling water and cook for 3 minutes. Rinse well in cold water and drain thoroughly. Set aside until needed.

Heat beef broth until simmering. Heat a dry wok, add beef, onion, garlic, soy sauce and sesame oil and stir fry until meat is cooked. Add mixture to the beef broth and simmer for 10 minutes.

Add cooked noodles, bean sprouts and dumplings and cook for a further 1 to 2 minutes until dumplings are warmed through. Divide among 4 bowls and scatter with spring onion. Serve with chopsticks and spoons.

Serves four.

Mu chungol

Yet another variation on beef and noodle soup, but one with a gentle, homely, unassuming quality more suited to a family dinner than a restaurant. If Koreans ever attempted to make minestrone, the end result would probably look like this.

2 eggs
2 tbsp peanut oil
1 onion, cut into slivers lengthwise
200 g (7 oz) daikon (white radish), cut into matchsticks
1 small zucchini, cut into matchsticks
200 g (7 oz) rump or sirloin steak, cut into matchsticks
2 litres (3½ pts) Korean beef broth (see Basics, page 193)
½ tsp salt
pinch of pepper
2 tsp sesame oil
2 cakes fresh tofu, cut into small cubes
2 spring onions, cut into 5 cm (2 in) slivers
150 g (5 oz) dang myun noodles

Beat eggs lightly. Heat 1 tablespoon oil in a hot wok and swirl around to coat surface. Pour in beaten egg and quickly swirl around the pan to form a thin omelette. When cooked on one side, gently separate the edge of the omelette from the wok with a knife. Place a plate over the wok and invert the whole thing so that the omelette drops onto the plate. Slide the omelette back in and quickly cook the other side. Roll up into a tight roll, slice across into thin strips and set aside.

In a large saucepan, heat remaining oil and fry onion for 2 minutes. Add white radish and zucchini and fry for a further 2 minutes. Add beef and fry for 1 minute. Pour in stock, season with salt, pepper and sesame oil. Add tofu and simmer for 5 to 6 minutes, carefully skimming off any froth that rises to the surface. Add spring onion during the last minute.

Meanwhile, cook noodles in boiling water for about 3 minutes. Drain and cut up with a few snips of the kitchen scissors. Divide among 4 large soup bowls. Pour soup, beef and vegetables over noodles. Sprinkle with omelette strips and serve with chopsticks and spoons.

Serves four.

Mul naeng myun

This popular Korean dish owes a lot to chilled Japanese buckwheat noodle dishes, such as Zaru soba and, indeed, soba noodles can be substituted here. One of the real joys about eating this dish in Korea is the meticulous and eye-catching arrangement of the ingredients on top of the noodles, practically an art form in its own right.

300 g (10 oz) naeng myun or soba
2 litres (3½ pts) Korean beef broth (see Basics, page 193), chilled
2 long green chillies, cut into thin strips
½ quantity Korean daikon pickles (see Basics, page 193)
½ quantity Korean cucumber pickles (see Basics, page 193)
24 thin slices cooked beef (from beef used to make the broth)
2 hard-boiled eggs, halved
1 tsp chilli flakes
hot mustard, vinegar and soy sauce, to serve

Cook noodles in a pot of simmering water for about 3 to 4 minutes until tender, rinse thoroughly in cold water, drain and chill.

When cold, divide noodles among 4 large, shallow bowls. Pour 1 to 2 cups of cold broth over each serving and carefully arrange strips of chilli, daikon pickles and cucumber pickles in neat little bundles on top of the noodles.

Fan out about 6 slices of meat on top, and top with half a hard-boiled egg, sprinkled with a little crushed chilli.

Serve with hot mustard, vinegar and soy sauce. Serve with chopsticks and spoons.

Serves four.

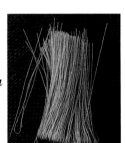

Spicy squid with somen

Somen are almost as popular in Korea as they are in Japan, but while the Japanese generally prefer to eat their somen cold with a subtle dipping sauce, the Koreans are far more adventurous and often throw them into powerful, almost rustic dishes such as this spicy stir fry.

150 g (5 oz) somen
500 g (1 lb) fresh squid, cleaned
2 tbsp peanut oil
2 tsp grated fresh ginger
2 cloves of garlic, finely chopped
1 small carrot, cut into thin matchsticks
1 onion, cut into slivers lengthwise
2 spring onions, finely sliced
¼ tsp salt
1 tsp sugar
1 tsp sesame oil
1 tsp sesame seeds, toasted
1 tbsp gochu jang chilli paste (from Korean or Japanese grocery stores)

Cook noodles for about 1 minute in a pot of boiling water. Drain and set aside.

Cut squid into strips about 1 cm (½ in) wide and 5 cm (2 in) long.

Heat peanut oil in a hot wok and fry ginger and garlic for 30 seconds. Add carrot and onion and stir fry for 4 minutes. Add squid and spring onion, salt and sugar and stir fry for a further minute.

Mix in sesame oil, sesame seeds and chilli paste. Combine with noodles, mixing thoroughly, and serve with chopsticks.

Serves four.

Korea　　*Noodle i-d **14***

Word of mouth

Lim Kueh Poh did not know that 14 February 1949 was going to be a special day. His friend, the *tung shu* almanac seller, had not given him any special dates; neither had the fortune-teller's little bird picked up any auspiciously numbered bamboo sticks.

As usual, he arrived at the corner of Trengganu and Temple Streets, deep in Singapore's Chinatown, at four o'clock in the afternoon. As usual, his body was bent under the weight of his portable kitchen which he carried as two loads on either end of his *kanda* stick. On one end hung his makeshift stove, hand-fashioned from a large oil drum, with its separate spaces for heating both the water and the broth. Spoons and chopsticks draped around its lid like a tribal necklace. On the other end hung a few stools and a large box-like affair which served as a makeshift table.

He set down his load in the shade of the covered five-foot-way, between Mr Yeo the knife sharpener and Leow Fook Hin, the *ting tang* man, who was, as usual, totally surrounded by noisy schoolchildren as he solemnly tapped away with his chisel and hammer, chipping away chunks of his jaw-breaking sugar and flour candy with a steady *ting tang, ting tang, ting tang*.

Lim started up the little charcoal fire under his stove. He set up the table and stools and, while waiting for the fire to take, sat down for a minute to listen to Lee Keng Boon, the storyteller across the road, reciting the *Golden Lotus of the Three Kingdoms* to a gossiping, smoking group of old men.

Soon, old Mr Chan, the barber, appeared at his doorway and shuffled up to Lim's stove. As usual, he bent over and peered into the now steaming stovetop with great curiosity, exclaiming, as if he had no idea of what lay within, 'Ahhhhh . . . laksa lemak.'

Lim immediately sprang into action. From a little compartment under the tabletop he produced a handful of thick white rice noodles which he immediately dropped into a wire strainer. Plunging the basket into the noodle water, he shook it up and down as if he were trying to shake some sense into it; lifting then plunging, lifting then plunging. Then a final lift, a shake, and a lightning flick of the wrist, and the noodles were snuggled up in a blue-and-white china bowl.

Lim opened a little metal drawer from within the table and produced two prawns, a little cooked chicken, a wedge of fried beancurd, a couple of cucumber slices and a handful of bean sprouts, all of which he deftly arranged on top of the noodles. Over that, he spooned a large ladle of creamy coconut soup.

Before long, five men – all regulars – were gathered around the table, eating laksa with a silent, powerful hunger. Their faces gave away nothing. Nobody ever said anything. They just paid their money, ate their soup and noodles, went away, and came back the next day to do it all over again. But on this particular day, a well-groomed young man Lim had never seen before approached the stove.

'Wonderful smell,' said the stranger. Lim sloshed the noodles, gathered the toppings and ladled the soup into the bowl. The young man picked up the bowl with two hands and held it up to his nose. 'Wah! Excellent! Your stock is very sound,' he said. 'Do I detect a trace of dried shrimp?' 'Yes, I do use dried shrimp,' said Lim, astonished. Nobody had ever talked to him about his laksa before. 'And a little ground *daun kesum*. Yes, very good,' said the young man to nobody in particular.

With every spoonful came another compliment. The words grew and blossomed like flowers from an Emperor's garden, and Lim felt a strange, heady pride that was alien and confusing and exciting all at once. The stranger shook Lim's hand. 'A laksa to be proud of,' he said, and walked across the road, past the storyteller.

That night, as Lim sat in his single bare room in Pagoda Street, pounding the *rempah* for tomorrow's laksa, he was still dizzy with good feelings. Determined to draw even more compliments from the stranger, he worked his paste finer and smoother than ever. He roasted his spices just a little longer than normal to draw out more of their essential oils.

But the stranger did not return. Instead, however, the old barber looked up from his bowl and grunted something about the aroma. Another regular, a teacher from the nearby school, passed a comment on his spicing. Another complimented his stock.

And so it went. The stranger never came back, but the compliments flowed like the Singapore River itself, and soon Lim's laksa lemak became so famous that even gourmets from Kuala Lumpur and Ipoh would stand in the long queue that inevitably snaked its way down Trengganu Street. The sweetness of his success put a spring in the old man's step, and he cooked with the energy of a child once again.

One day, as he arrived to set up his stall, he did something he hadn't done in years. He bought some candy from the *ting tang* man. As he turned to move away, he stopped, with his mouth full, and said, 'Very good. Very good candy.'

The *ting tang* man stopped chipping for a moment, not knowing what to make of such a comment, then resumed his steady rhythm. But there was a certain brightness to the *ting*, a higher note struck by the *tang*, that seemed to resonate in the air.

Ting tang, ting tang, ting tang.

Indonesia
Philippines
Burma
Taiwan
Laos
Cambodia
India

Bahmi goreng

This is the noodle equivalent of nasi goreng, or Indonesian fried rice. Like fried rice, it can accommodate whatever leftovers you have in the cupboard, so use this recipe as a guide. Indonesians like to serve it with extra kecap manis and chilli sauce on the side.

300 g (10 oz) dried egg noodles
3 tbsp peanut oil
2 eggs, beaten
2 cloves of garlic, crushed with the side of a knife blade
1 chicken breast, finely sliced
80 g (3 oz) pork fillet, finely sliced
80 g (3 oz) raw, peeled prawns
80 g (3 oz) Peking cabbage leaves, finely sliced
1 stalk of celery, finely sliced
4 spring onions, finely sliced
3 tbsp chicken stock
1 tbsp kecap manis
1 tbsp soy sauce
2 tbsp crisp-fried shallots (optional)

Cook noodles in boiling water for about 4 minutes, then rinse with cold water to stop them from cooking further. Drain and set aside.

Heat ½ tablespoon of oil in a hot wok and swirl around to coat surface. Pour in beaten egg and quickly swirl around the pan to form a thin omelette. When cooked on one side, gently separate the edge of the omelette from the wok with a knife. Place a plate over the wok and invert the whole thing so that the omelette drops onto the plate. Slide the omelette back in and quickly cook the other side. Roll up into a tight roll, slice across into thin strips and set aside.

Heat remaining oil in the wok and fry garlic, chicken and pork until they have changed colour, for only a minute or two. Add prawns, cabbage, celery and spring onion and toss well. Add stock, kecap manis, soy sauce and drained noodles and mix well. Tip onto a large serving platter and scatter omelette strips and crisp-fried shallots, if using, over the top.

Serves four.

Indonesia   *Noodle i-d* **2**

Soto ayam

A full-bodied, aromatic dish that's halfway between a curry and a soup, this is a popular lunch and family dinner in both Indonesia and Malaysia. The addition of noodles makes it a great party dish. If your prefer more of a chew, you could use bean thread vermicelli instead of rice vermicelli.

1 chicken, about 1.2 kg (2 lb)
1 tsp salt
1 tsp black peppercorns
4 candlenuts, crushed
1 stalk of lemongrass, white heart only, finely sliced
2 cloves of garlic, peeled
6 shallots, peeled
1 tsp ginger, grated
2 thin slices of galangal, chopped
1 tsp ground coriander
½ tsp ground turmeric
1 tsp ground cumin
2 tbsp peanut oil
200 g (7 oz) rice vermicelli
2 potatoes, boiled, peeled and diced
1 cup bean sprouts
2 hard-boiled eggs, sliced
¼ cup fresh coriander leaves
2 tbsp crisp-fried shallots (available from Asian grocery stores)

Put chicken in a pot with a snug-fitting lid and add just enough water, about 2 litres (3½ pts) to cover. Add salt and peppercorns and bring to the boil. Skim off any froth that rises to the surface, reduce heat, and simmer, partly covered, until the chicken is cooked, about 45 minutes. Allow chicken and stock to cool, then shred meat and set aside. Reserve stock.

Using a mortar and pestle, grind candlenuts, lemongrass, garlic, shallots, ginger, galangal, coriander, turmeric and cumin to a paste. Heat oil in a saucepan and fry the paste over gentle heat for about 5 minutes. Pour in the reserved chicken stock, cover and simmer for 10 minutes.

Pour boiling water over noodles and let stand for 6 to 7 minutes. Drain, then transfer to a saucepan of boiling water and cook for one more minute. Rinse in cold water. Drain well and cut into short lengths with a pair of scissors. Place some noodles into each soup bowl. Add chicken meat and diced potato to the soup, and warm through for 2 minutes. Pour soup over the noodles and garnish with bean sprouts, egg slices, fresh coriander leaves and a sprinkling of crisp-fried shallots.

Serves four.

Pancit canton

If you can't find pancit canton, Chinese e-fu noodles will do just as well – the difference between the two is minimal. This simple, no-fuss stir fry is really just the Filipino version of chow mein and is a popular lunchtime eat-and-run dish.

2 tbsp peanut oil
1 onion, finely sliced into rings
2 cloves of garlic, finely chopped
1 cup char sieu (red roast pork), cut into thin strips
¼ cabbage, thinly sliced
1 carrot, cut into thin matchsticks
1 large stalk of celery, cut into thin matchsticks
2 tbsp light soy sauce
¼ tsp salt
½ tsp sugar
pinch of pepper
1 cup small raw prawns or shrimps, peeled
1½ cups chicken stock
200 g (7 oz) pancit canton
2 lemons, cut into wedges

Heat oil in a hot wok and cook onion rings for 3 minutes. Add garlic and cook just until it starts to colour. Add pork, cabbage, carrot, celery, 1 tablespoon soy sauce, salt, sugar and pepper. Cook, stirring, for about 5 minutes, then add prawns and cook for another 2 minutes. Remove mixture from wok.

Put stock and remaining soy sauce in the wok and heat through. Add noodles, stirring gently until they soften and 'melt down' into the stock. When they have absorbed about half the liquid, add the stir-fry mixture. When noodles feel cooked (another 1 or 2 minutes), transfer to a large, warm serving platter and toss well. Serve with lemon wedges.

Serves four.

Mohinga

Even people who know nothing about Burmese cooking, or Burma for that matter, seem to have heard of *mohinga*. This robust, full-bodied dish is present at most festivals, celebrations and even formal dinner parties. To call it a curried fish soup with noodles is to miss the point totally.

750 g (1½ lb) thick, white-fleshed fish cutlets
2 stalks of lemongrass, split in half
4 slices ginger, 2.5 cm (1 in) square
2 onions, finely chopped
1 chilli, split
2 tbsp fish sauce
4 cloves of garlic
1 tbsp grated ginger
1 tsp shrimp paste
1 tsp ground turmeric
1 stalk of lemongrass, white part only, sliced
2 chillies, chopped
3 tbsp peanut oil
2 tbsp chickpea flour (besan)
1 tbsp rice flour
2½ cups coconut milk
¼ Peking cabbage, shredded
2 tbsp lime juice
1 tsp salt
1 tsp sugar
200 g (7 oz) rice vermicelli
lime wedges, crisp-fried onions and chilli flakes, to serve

Put fish in a saucepan and cover with cold water. Add split lemongrass, ginger, half the onion, split chilli, and fish sauce.

Simmer, covered, for 10 minutes. Carefully lift out fish and reserve. Strain stock and set aside. Using a mortar and pestle, pound garlic, grated ginger, shrimp paste, turmeric, sliced lemongrass and chopped chilli to a paste.

In a pan, heat the oil and cook the remaining chopped onion until soft and golden. Add the paste and fry for 4 or 5 minutes, until aromatic.

Remove bones and skin from fish and add fish to the spice mixture. Add 3 cups of the strained fish stock. Mix a little stock with the chickpea and rice flours to form a creamy mixture, and stir this into the soup. Add coconut milk and simmer for a further 5 minutes. Add shredded cabbage and cook until it is tender. Add lime juice, salt and sugar to taste.

Boil the rice vermicelli briefly for 2 minutes. Drain and divide noodles among 4 serving bowls. Ladle curry over the noodles. Serve with additional lime wedges, crisp-fried onions, and chilli flakes.

Serves four.

Panthe kaukswe

Like Burma itself, these aromatic, curried noodles draw heavily on the cultures of India and China. Traditionally, the dish is made with a type of bean thread noodle known as *pekyasan*, but thin egg noodles give the dish more substance.

3 onions, chopped
3 cloves of garlic, chopped
2 chillies, chopped
1 tbsp finely chopped ginger
1 tsp chilli powder
2 tsp ground cumin
1 tsp ground coriander
2 tsp ground turmeric
3 tbsp peanut oil
1.5 kg (3 lb) chicken, cut into 8 pieces
1 cinnamon stick
2 litres (3½ pts) chicken stock
3 tbsp chickpea flour (besan)
½ cup water
3 cups thick coconut milk
2 tbsp fish sauce
300 g (10 oz) fresh egg noodles

Using a mortar and pestle, pound the onion, garlic, chilli, ginger, chilli powder, cumin, coriander and turmeric powder to a paste.

Heat oil in a pan and cook spice paste for about 5 minutes, until aromatic. Add chicken pieces and fry for a couple of minutes, coating the pieces well with the spice mix. Add cinnamon stick, pour on chicken stock and simmer, covered, for 35 minutes. Remove chicken pieces, take the meat from the bones, and return meat to the pan.

Mix the chickpea flour and water and stir into the pan. Add the coconut milk and simmer for 15 minutes. Stir in fish sauce.

Cook the noodles in boiling water for about 1 minute, drain and arrange on a large serving platter. Transfer curry to a separate platter. Serve with a mixture of condiments for adding to the curry, including crisp-fried garlic cloves, quartered hard-boiled eggs, lemon wedges, coriander sprigs, crushed dried chilli briefly stir fried in peanut oil, and crisp, deep-fried rice noodles.

Serves four.

Burma   *Noodle i-d* **2**

Stir-fried pumpkin with rice vermicelli

The Taiwanese love their noodles, although most of their favourites are variations of Hunanese, Sichuanese and Shanghainese noodle dishes. Pumpkin is rarely used in noodle dishes throughout Asia. After tasting this dish, you'll wonder why.

500 g (1 lb) clams
½ cup water
300 g (10 oz) rice vermicelli
200 g (7 oz) pumpkin, peeled
1 tbsp peanut oil
2 spring onions, finely sliced
3 tbsp dried shrimp, soaked for 30 minutes and drained
1 cup chicken stock
½ tsp sesame oil
½ tsp salt
½ tsp sugar
¼ tsp white pepper

To cook clams, heat water in a lidded frypan until boiling. Add clams and cover tightly. Cook over high heat for 1 minute, then remove all opened clams with tongs. Cook for 1 minute more and remove all opened clams. Discard water, and keep clams in a covered bowl.

Place rice noodles in heatproof bowl and cover with boiling water. Leave to stand for 6 to 7 minutes, then drain. Rinse under cold water, drain again and set aside.

Cut pumpkin into fine matchsticks. Heat oil in a hot wok and cook spring onion and shrimp for 1 minute. Add pumpkin and stir fry for another 30 seconds. Add stock and simmer for 10 minutes, or until pumpkin is soft and tender. Add rice noodles and toss well until heated through. Add clams, sesame oil, salt, sugar and white pepper, and serve.

Serves four.

Khao pun nam ya

Most Laotian noodle dishes seem to be re-takes on Thai dishes, and while this one often travels under its Thai name of khanom jeen ya, the sauce is typical of Laotian fish cookery. If you want to make the dish more authentically Laotian, double the number of chillies.

4 dried chillies, soaked overnight and drained
1 stalk of lemongrass, white part only, finely sliced
2 slices galangal, chopped
4 cloves of garlic, finely chopped
6 shallots, peeled and chopped
2 tbsp nam pla ra (see Basics, page 191)
1 tbsp fish sauce
2½ cups water
500 g (1 lb) boned fish (e.g. tuna, bream, snapper)
2½ cups coconut milk
½ tsp salt
2 tsp sugar
6 kaffir lime leaves
400 g (14 oz) fresh round rice noodles (khanom jeen), or
    300 g (10 oz) rice vermicelli, cooked and drained
½ carrot, sliced into thin matchsticks
2 cups bean sprouts
2 fresh red chillies, finely sliced
½ cup finely shredded Tientsin cabbage
1 cup loosely packed mint leaves

Using a mortar and pestle, pound chillies, lemongrass, galangal, garlic and shallot to a smooth paste. In a saucepan, combine the nam pla ra, fish sauce and water. Gently poach fish until cooked through. Strain stock and set aside.

Flake fish and lightly pound to a coarse, lumpy paste.

In another saucepan, heat 1 cup coconut milk, stirring, and simmer until it evaporates and forms an oily cream. Add spice paste and stir fry until it is warm and fragrant. Add fish, stirring well, and cook for another minute or two. Moisten with a little of the fish stock until it is not quite runny.

In another saucepan, heat remaining stock, remaining coconut milk, salt, sugar and lime leaves. Cook gently for 3 or 4 minutes.

Place noodles in a colander or strainer and pour boiling water over until warmed through. Drain well and divide noodles among 4 soup bowls. Add carrot, bean sprouts, sliced chilli and cabbage, and pour on the coconut broth, not quite covering the noodles. Ladle a big scoop of the fish 'mush' on top of the noodles, and garnish with mint leaves.

Serves four.

Laos   *Noodle i-d* **9**

Pork and rice stick noodle soup

This is a real one-pot wonder, combining fish balls, prawns, squid and pork in an easy-going family-style soup. In Cambodia, the dish would be made with pure pork stock, but I prefer to use chicken stock to lighten it and give it a little more subtlety.

500 g (1 lb) belly pork or leg pork
2.5 litres (4½ pts) pork or chicken stock
1 tbsp dried shrimp
2 cloves of garlic, finely chopped
½ tsp salt
½ tsp sugar
1 squid, cleaned
8 fish balls
8 green prawns, peeled
400 g (14 oz) dried thin rice stick noodles
1 tbsp fish sauce
¼ cup coriander leaves
¼ cup chopped spring onion greens
1 red chilli, sliced
2 cups loosely packed bean sprouts, washed
1 lemon, quartered, to serve

Put pork, stock, dried shrimp, garlic, salt and sugar in a large saucepan and bring to the boil. Skim off any froth that rises to the surface, reduce heat and simmer, covered, for 1 hour. Remove pork, slice thinly, and set aside.

Cut squid into pieces about 5 cm (2 in) square. Score the underside of each piece in a diamond pattern. Cut fish balls in half. Devein prawns by hooking out the black intestinal tract with a fine bamboo skewer.

Cook noodles in plenty of boiling water for about 4 minutes and drain well. Divide them among 4 big soup bowls and top with 5 or 6 pork slices.

Bring stock back to the boil, add prawns, squid and fish balls, and leave for about 1 minute. Add fish sauce, then immediately ladle soup and seafood over the noodles and pork. Scatter with coriander leaves and spring onion, and serve with a side plate of sliced chilli, bean sprouts and lemon quarters.

Serves four.

Sevian kheer

This sweet noodle and milk pudding is particularly popular in northern India and Pakistan, and is a favourite of Muslims, who traditionally eat it after moonrise during Ramadan. If you're lucky, you might be able to find the true sevian in an Indian food store, but traditional Italian vermicelli will also work, as long as it is very fine.

4 tbsp ghee
⅓ cup cashew nuts
⅓ cup blanched almonds, roughly chopped
⅓ cup pistachio nuts, roughly chopped
150 g (5 oz) sevian or thin Italian vermicelli,
    broken into 5 cm (2 in) pieces
1.25 litres (2 pts) milk
½ tsp ground cardamom
⅓ cup sultanas
3 tbsp sugar
2 tsp rosewater
extra pistachio nuts, chopped, for decoration
a few unsprayed rose petals, washed and dried, for decoration

Heat ghee in a heavy pan and fry cashews, almonds and pistachios over medium heat just until they start to colour.

Add vermicelli and fry, being careful not to let the noodles brown. As soon as they turn golden, pour in milk and bring to a simmer. Add cardamom and sultanas and simmer for 15 minutes.

Add sugar and rosewater and warm through until sugar has dissolved. Serve in individual bowls, sprinkled with extra chopped pistachios and rose petals. Serve hot, or leave to cool and serve at room temperature.

Serves four.

India　　　　*Noodle i-d* **6**

Crossing the bridge

One of the wisest, richest and most respected men in all of Yunan had a problem so deep and so wretched that even his untold riches and vast wisdom could not begin to solve it.

The problem was the man's son. Not that he wasn't a loving and respectful son, for he was all this and more. The problem was the boy's inability to pass the Imperial Exams. In Yunan, in those ancient times, not passing the Imperial Exams was akin to not passing Life itself. Time after time, the boy would sit for the precious exams, and time after time, he would fail.

He was not a stupid boy, reasoned his father. He was merely too easily distracted, that was all. Because the world contained so many things to be fascinated by, the boy found himself lured into pursuing them rather than pursuing the studies that separated a rich, fulfilled and meaningful future from a wastrel's past.

Determined that his son would fail neither the exams nor his family, the father swore that the boy would have one last attempt at passing the exams, and this time there would be no distractions. He ordered his son to leave the family residence and to move all his belongings to the one-room garden cottage located on a small island in a pond at the back of the house. Only a single wooden bridge led to the island, and the father made it quite clear that under no circumstances was the boy to cross the bridge until his studies were completed.

This was the cause of great pain to the family cook, who treasured the boy almost as much as he treasured the art of cooking and pleasing people with his food. The island was a long way from the kitchen and the winds that hurled their way through the mountains from the rugged west were at their coldest and cruellest at this time of the year.

Whatever noble dish he created, however much care and time and love he lavished on its preparation, was for nothing, for the dish would be as cold and as unfeeling as a pebble on the bottom of the pond by the time he crossed that cursed bridge. Plates came back untouched, dumplings came back unbroken, and soups came back unsipped.

But the good cook persevered nevertheless, taking more breathtaking creations across the bridge, only to see them stripped of their purpose and being by the wicked, unfeeling winds.

Then one day, the cook's hands danced and darted above the work bench as if guided by a kind, invisible god. He assembled all of his young master's favourite foods – white silvery fish plucked from the river that very day, a marbled slice of chicken breast taken from the proudest bird in the yard, and shrimps that shone like pearls in the moonlight.

With his oldest and most trusted cleaver he cut them into slices that were so thin and even, they were as clear and as transparent as a mountain stream. He assembled all of these on one plate, then cooked up a serving of fine egg noodles, the very same noodles he had fed to the boy when he was struck down by fever at the age of three.

'The best noodles I have ever tasted,' said the boy at the time, and the cook felt a burning pride every time he remembered those words. Then he prepared a broth from the aforesaid chicken and flavoured it with precious rice wine, *choy sum* leaves and minced ginger. He stoked the fire under the stove until it burned with a fury, and the soup bubbled and spluttered as if it had been ambushed.

Without daring even to breathe, lest his breath cooled the potion, the cook ladled the still-bubbling soup into a warm tureen, then ever so carefully poured in a ladleful of molten chicken fat that slithered over the surface of the soup like a grand silken robe slipping over the body of its master.

Quickly, the cook placed all the bowls on the household's finest and most embellished tray and set off over the bridge, chuckling all the way. The maids and servants watched him curiously, for they were not to know that what he was really chuckling at was the wind.

Arriving at the cottage, he summoned the boy to the table and commanded him to place the noodles, the fish, the meat and the prawns into the soup. The boy did so without appetite and with more than a little annoyance. He dug his spoon into the bowl and placed it into his mouth with flat, motionless eyes. Suddenly, he let out a yelp that carried over the pond like a frightened frog's call.

'It is too hot!' he said, and began laughing. 'I know,' said the cook, nodding happily. 'It is the chicken fat that keeps out the wind, the cold, and the bad spirits. Now that you have the nourishment you need, learning will come naturally and gracefully.'

The boy ate the delicious soup with a hunger that he didn't know he had, as he watched the cook skipping like a child across the bridge back to his kitchen.

Some weeks later, the exams were held and the boy, of course, passed. Which meant he could fruitfully spend the rest of his life being forever distracted by the world and its wonders.

Basics

Homemade egg noodles

2 cups sifted plain flour
2 eggs
½ tsp salt
1 tsp corn or peanut oil
3 tbsp water
extra flour, for dusting

Sift flour onto a wooden or marble surface and make a well in the centre. Add eggs, salt, oil and water and, with the tips of your fingers, start to draw the flour into the wet ingredients. Keep mixing, slowly tumbling the flour into the liquid until a rough, crumbly mixture is formed. Keep on working until a rough dough ball forms.

Knead dough, stretching it firmly and slapping down hard on the work bench for 5 to 10 minutes until it is smooth, lump-free and shiny. If the dough starts to feel sticky, sprinkle a little more flour around. If it is dry and crumbly, wet your hands with water and keep working. Cover with plastic wrap and leave to rest for about 2 hours.

Cut dough in quarters. Squash the first piece down with the palm of your hand and thread in through a pasta machine on the widest setting. Sprinkle the sheet with a little flour, then thread it through again. Reduce the setting one notch and thread through twice more. When the dough sheet gets too long to handle easily, cut it in half. Keep reducing the thickness until the noodle sheet is the required thickness.

Feed the sheets through the cutting blade, choosing the size of noodle that's right for the dish.

Use immediately or sprinkle with a little flour and spread out on a tray to dry out.

Makes enough to serve four.

Homemade udon

2 egg yolks
1½ cups water
1 tbsp salt
1 kg (2 lb) sifted plain flour

Beat egg yolks and mix with water and salt. Make a well in the centre of the flour with your hands and pour in the liquid. With the tips of your fingers, gradually work in the flour and slowly but steadily amalgamate the ingredients thoroughly until they form a dough ball that holds together. Knead the dough, using all your strength, for about 10 minutes, until the dough is completely smooth with a satiny sheen to its surface. The dough should feel firm, but malleable. If it is too sloppy, sprinkle with a little more flour; if it is too dry, moisten your hands with water and continue to work. Wrap in clingwrap and leave to rest for an hour or two.

Dust a board or marble slab with flour and, using a wooden rolling pin, roll the dough out to a rectangle. Keep rolling until the dough is around ½ cm (¼ in) thick. Sprinkle dough with flour and fold it backwards and forwards on itself three times so that the edges look like one and a half 'S's. Lay the folded dough on the board and, with a very sharp knife, cut across the folds in strips, just under ½ cm (¼ in) wide.

Insert a long chopstick or a piece of wooden rod into the middle fold, then lift up to reveal your freshly made noodles.

Makes enough to serve eight.

Homemade soba

600 g (19 oz) buckwheat flour
400 g (14 oz) plain flour
2 cups water.

Put the flours in a large work bowl. With a circular motion, mix them together with your hands, while at the same time tipping in the water, a little at a time, with the other hand. Work rapidly, amalgamating the water and flour with your fingers. You should have poured in about three-quarters of the water in a minute. Reserve remaining water. Use the fingers and palms of both hands to feel your way through the dough pressing it and moving it on. Grab a clump of dough in your hands, press firmly then allow the dough clumps to fall back into the bowl. Keep working in this manner for about 3 minutes. Add remaining water and work for another minute or two.

Now it's time for some heavy kneading action. Lean heavily into the bowl, using the weight of your body, and push down on the dough, pressing it together. Keep kneading and rolling the dough until it forms a smooth ball.

Wrap dough in plastic wrap and leave to rest for an hour or two.

Cut dough in quarters. Sprinkle some buckwheat flour on a board or marble slab and press down with the palm of your hand to flatten the ball a little. Using a rolling pin, roll it out to an oval about 0.5 cm (¼ in) thick. Sprinkle some buckwheat flour over dough and cut in half. Lay both halves on top of each other, matching the cut edges, then fold them upon themselves. Starting at the flat edge, cut the dough with a sharp knife into strips 0.5 cm (¼ in) wide. Place noodles on a tray and sprinkle with flour. They are now ready to use.

Makes enough to serve eight.

Chinese chicken stock

2 kg (4½ lb) chicken bones, necks, wings, feet, etc.
200 g (7 oz) chunk of ham
4 spring onions, white part only
3 thick slices ginger
2 onions, quartered

Wash bones well in cold water, then place in a pot with 3 to 3.5 litres (5½ to 6 pts) of water. Add ham, spring onions, ginger and onion, and bring to the boil. Skim off the froth that forms on the surface, reduce heat and simmer, partly covered, for 1 hour. Allow to cool, then strain and refrigerate.

Sichuan chilli oil

1 cup peanut oil
3 tbsp dried red chillies, crushed
1 teaspoon Sichuan peppercorns

Heat oil in a wok until almost smoking, then turn off heat. Add chilli and peppercorns and leave to cool. Strain through muslin or a fine sieve into a screw-top bottle and store in a cool, dark place.

Char sieu (Red roast pork)

1.2 kg (2½ lb) pork neck (from Asian butcher) or boneless pork

Marinade:
1 tsp salt
4 tbsp soy sauce
4 slices of ginger, peeled
3 tbsp maltose (from Asian food stores) or honey, warmed
2 tbsp white sugar
2 cloves of garlic, crushed with the side of a knife blade
2 tbsp shaohsing rice wine, or dry sherry
1 level tsp five-spice powder
2 tbsp hoisin sauce
pinch of red food colouring (annatto seeds) (optional)

For basting:
4 tbsp honey, warmed

Cut pork lengthwise into 3 equal strips, roughly 4 cm (1½ in) thick and 18 cm (7 in) long. Combine marinade incredients in a large bowl or pan and add pork. Leave to marinate for 6 hours, or overnight, remembering to turn the meat over every now and then.

Preheat oven to 200°C (400°F) and roast for 20 minutes with meat lying flat on a wire rack set high in the oven. Place a roasting pan with 1 cm (½ in) water underneath to catch the drips. After 20 minutes, turn pork over and brush with warmed honey. Leave for 15 minutes more, then turn and brush with honey again, and roast for a final 15 minutes. The pork should have nicely charred edges, but watch that it doesn't burn too much. To serve, slice finely across the grain.

Golden omelette strips

1 tbsp peanut oil
2 eggs, lightly beaten

Heat oil in a hot wok and swirl around to coat surface. Pour in beaten egg and quickly swirl around the pan to form a thin omelette. When cooked on one side, gently separate the edge of the omelette from the wok with a knife. Place a plate over the wok and invert the whole thing so that the omelette drops onto the plate. Slide the omelette back in and quickly cook the other side. Roll up into a tight roll and slice across into thin strips.

Laksa paste

1 onion, finely chopped
1 tbsp ginger, grated
1 tbsp galangal, grated
2 cloves of garlic, chopped
2 stalks of lemongrass, white part only, sliced
6 dried chillies, soaked and chopped
4 candlenuts or macadamia nuts, crushed
1 tbsp blachan (shrimp paste)
6 laksa leaves (Vietnamese mint)
1 tsp turmeric
1 tsp ground coriander
1 tsp paprika
1 tsp ground cumin

Using a mortar and pestle, pound ingredients to a thick, fragrant, amalgamated paste. Alternatively, blend in food processor, adding ingredients gradually.

Fresh coconut milk

Unless you have a rotary coconut grater (available from Indian and Asian stores), you may well be doomed to a life of canned coconut milk. If you do find one, here's what to do:

Hold a coconut in the palm of your hand and give it a sharp thwack with the back of a cleaver or a hammer. Turn the coconut around in your hand and continue to thwack along the circumference line until it breaks in half.

Pour off the clear juice and, using your grater, grate away all the coconut flesh. Place the flesh in a bowl, cover with hot water and let stand for 10 minutes. Squeeze the flesh through a sieve, a fine cloth, or a clean linen tea-towel into another bowl, add a little salt, and leave to stand for 30 minutes. The thicker cream will rise to the top, leaving the thinner milk below.

Use on the same day as grating.

Dashi

1 litre (2 pts) cold water
piece of konbu (kelp) 7.5 cm (3 in) square
25 g (1 oz) dried bonito flakes

Put water in a pot, add konbu and heat. Just before water begins to boil, remove kelp and add bonito flakes. Bring back to the boil, then instantly remove pot from heat. After 30 seconds to 1 minute, strain though muslin or a fine sieve and cool until required.

Alternatively, you could use instant dashi powder, mixing 1 litre (1¾ pts) boiling water with 15 g (½ oz) of powder and simmering for 2 to 3 minutes.

Tempura batter

2 egg yolks
2 cups iced water
2 cups sifted flour

Put egg yolks in a bowl, add iced water and mix lightly with chopsticks without beating. Add flour, all at once, and mix lightly with chopsticks until rough and lumpy. Don't overmix or the batter will be heavy.

Nam pla ra

(Fish sauce for use in Thai and Laotian recipes)
2 fillets of pickled mudfish (sold in jars in Thai grocery stores as
    pickled gourami)
3 cups water
1 lime
3 shallots
1 stalk of lemongrass, white part only, crushed

Combine all ingredients in a saucepan and bring to the boil. Simmer, half covered, for about 30 minutes, or until fish has fallen apart. Strain and reserve.

Thai red curry paste

10 dried red chillies
1 tbsp coriander seeds
1 tsp cumin seeds
6 white peppercorns
2 slices galangal, finely chopped
2 stalks of lemongrass, white part only, finely chopped
1 tablespoon chopped coriander root
4 tbsp chopped shallot
1 tsp shrimp paste
1 tsp kaffir lime peel, finely chopped
4 cloves of garlic, chopped
1 tsp salt

Soak chillies in warm water for 30 minutes. Drain and chop finely.

Roast coriander seeds and cumin seeds in a dry, hot frying pan for about 3 minutes until they just start to colour and release their aromas. Using a mortar and pestle, slowly pound all the ingredients together. Keep working until a nice, moist paste is formed.

Makes ½ cup.

191

Nuoc cham (Vietnamese dipping sauce)

2 red chillies, sliced
2 cloves of garlic, peeled and chopped
1 tsp sugar
juice of 1 lime
1 tbsp white vinegar
1 tbsp water
3 tbsp fish sauce

Using a mortar and pestle, pound chilli with garlic. Add sugar, lime juice, vinegar, water and fish sauce. Serve in small individual bowls.

Mandu dumplings

250 g (8 oz) minced beef
100 g (3 oz) kimchi cabbage, squeezed dry and finely chopped
50 g (2 oz) bean sprouts, blanched and finely chopped
50 g (2 oz) fresh tofu, squeezed dry through muslin
3 spring onions, white part only, finely chopped
1 tsp sesame oil
2 tsp sesame seeds, toasted
1 egg yolk
2 tsp cornflour
1 cm (½ in) piece ginger, grated
salt and pepper to taste
1 pack shoei jeau pastry rounds, or round wonton wrappers
3 litres (5 pts) Korean beef broth (see Basics, page 193)

For dumplings, combine all ingredients, except pastry and beef broth, in a bowl and mix together well with your hands. Take 2 teaspoons of filling and roll it into a ball. Continue rolling balls of filling until the mixture is used up. Arrange the balls on a tray, cover with plastic wrap and refrigerate for 1 hour.

Wet the edge of a dumpling wrapper with a little water and place a dumpling in the middle. Pull the edges over the filling to form a semi-circle, and pleat the curved edge together to seal it tightly.

Bring broth to the boil, put 6 dumplings into the broth and simmer for a few minutes until the filling feels firm to the touch. Remove and cook 6 more. The dumplings can be frozen.

Makes about thirty.

Korean beef broth

5 litres (9 pts) water
1.5 kg (3 lb) beef bones
2 kg (4½ lb) beef (chuck or brisket)
2 teaspoons salt
1 large onion, cut into 8 pieces
5 cm (2 in) knob of ginger, sliced into 4 or 5 pieces
5 cloves of garlic, crushed with the side of a knife blade
1½ teaspoons black peppercorns
4 tablespoons soy sauce

Place water, bones, beef and salt in a large saucepan and bring to the boil. Reduce heat and simmer, skimming carefully for 10 minutes or so until the scum stops forming. Add onion, ginger, garlic, peppercorns and soy sauce and simmer, partly covered, for about 3 hours.

Remove beef and reserve. Strain broth through your finest sieve and store overnight in the refrigerator. When chilled, remove fat that accumulates on the top. Strain off the quantity needed for the dish, and freeze remaining stock in convenient portions for future use.

Korean cucumber pickles

1½ teaspoons salt
1 tablespoon sugar
2½ tablespoons rice vinegar
2 small pickling cucumbers

Combine salt, sugar and vinegar in a small bowl and mix well. Slice cucumber into thin matchsticks about 5 to 6 cm (2 to 2½ in) long. Add cucumber, cover with plastic wrap and leave to stand for about 3 hours before refrigerating.

Korean daikon pickles

400 g (14 oz) daikon (white radish), peeled
1 teaspoon dried crushed chilli
3 cloves of garlic, crushed with the side of a knife blade
1 small knob of ginger, crushed with the side of a knife blade

Cut daikon into thick matchsticks about 4 cm (1½ in) long and 1 cm (½ in) thick and toss on a slightly curved plate with chilli, garlic and ginger. Place a small flat plate on top and weigh down with a large can. Leave to sit for 3 to 4 hours before refrigerating.

Glossary

Aburage Flat, golden, deep-fried bean curd cakes, sold frozen in Japanese food stores. These are particularly popular in Fox noodles (*kitsune udon*, page 98).

Asian basil Similar to the Italian variety but more pungent and more predominantly aniseed in flavour. Asian basil is very popular in Thailand where three main varieties are used: *horatha*, which looks like sweet basil, only smaller; holy basil or *kaprao*, which is used in more powerful dishes; and lemon basil, known as *manglak*, which is hairy in appearance.

Bean curd puffs Deep-fried cubes of bean curd, sold in plastic packets in the refrigerated section of Asian supermarkets.

Belacan, also called blachan Dried shrimp paste made from salted and fermented dried shrimp. Widely used in Malaysian cooking, its pungent smell and flavour are both acquired tastes. Known as *terasi* in Indonesia, *kapi* in Thailand and *mam tom* in Vietnam.

Black fungus see wood ear fungus

Bonito flakes Steam-cooked bonito fish are dried and then shaved into paper-thin flakes. With konbu seaweed and water, bonito flakes form dashi, an all-purpose stock that is one of the staples of Japanese cooking.

Brown bean sauce Also known as bean sauce, yellow bean sauce and *taucheo* in Malaysia. It is made from fermented soy beans and is available in glass jars or cans. See also yellow bean sauce.

Cabbage, bak choy Often just called Chinese cabbage, this popular Chinese green has large white celery-like stalks and dark green leaves that resemble spinach.

Cabbage, choy sum Known as flowering cabbage because of its distinctive yellow flowers. It can be steamed, poached or stir fried.

Cabbage, Peking Also known as Tientsin cabbage, *wong nga baak* and Chinese leaves in England, it is a long, pale cabbage similar in colour and texture to the Savoy cabbage.

Candlenut A round nut, similar to a macadamia, used to thicken and add a sweet nutty flavour to Thai and Malaysian dishes.

Char sieu Glazed barbecued pork sold in Chinese barbecued meat shops, where it can be seen hanging in glossy hanks.

Chickpea flour (besan) A flour made by grinding small brown chickpeas, besan is used in Indonesia and Malysia as a thickening agent.

Chilli bean sauce Similar to brown bean sauce, but fired up with the addition of chilli. This sauce is particularly popular in Sichuan and is a must-have ingredient for *ma po* bean curd.

Chilli sambal, sambal oelek A popular spicy sauce from Indonesia made with cooked red chillies and soy sauce.

Chilli sauce, sweet A thick, sweetened chilli sauce favoured in Thai cooking. A similar sauce is used in Malaysia but it tends to be hotter and less sweet.

Chinese mushrooms (shiitake) see Mushrooms, shiitake

Coconut cream A thick liquid made by combining grated coconut with hot water, and squeezing out the residue (see Basics, page 190). It is readily available in cans, which are far more convenient, although the taste and texture of fresh coconut cream is incomparable – rather like comparing fresh clotted cream with evaporated milk.

Cornflour, cornstarch The classic Chinese thickener. Used sparingly, it is a valuable friend. Be heavy handed with it, and you'll turn everything into instant glug. Never mix with hot water, only cold. Try mixing it with rice wine or another liquid already in the recipe.

Crisp-fried shallots Golden brown, crisp, deep-fried shallot pieces are sold in airtight jars in Asian food stores. They are much loved in Malaysian cooking. Fried onions and fried garlic are also available.

Cucumber, Japanese or Lebanese Smaller, crisper and drier than the cucumbers we are used to, these are sometimes found in Japanese stores. Very young common cucumbers can be substituted.

Curry leaves Available in both fresh and dried form, and used extensively in Malaysia, India and Burma.

Daikon radish Giant, white Japanese radish with a mild, refreshing flavour.

Dashi An essential ingredient for so much Japanese cooking, this subtle yet distinctive broth is made with konbu (kelp) and dried bonito (fish). Make your own (see Basics, page 191), or buy instant dashi sold in sachets packaged in little cardboard boxes. Mix 15 g (½ oz) instant dashi powder with 1 litre (1¾ pts) boiling water.

Dried red chillies Long, red, dried chillies sold in large plastic packets. They are usually soaked overnight before using and can be pounded to a paste for use in stir fries, soups and curries.

Dried shrimp Tiny, hard, sun-dried or air-dried shrimp are a feature in practically every Southeast Asian cuisine. They are usually soaked in water before use, or ground to a powder.

Fish balls Mainly used in soups, but they occasionally pop up in stir fries. These cooked balls of minced fish paste can be found in the refrigerated section of Asian food stores.

Fish sauce It might be a bit whiffy, but this dark, pungent, salty sauce made from fermented fish adds a distinctive flavour that is downright addictive. It is known as *nuoc mam* in Vietnam, *nam pla* in Thailand, and *patis* in the Philippines.

Galangal Sometimes called Siamese ginger, although it is not really a ginger. Also known as *laos*, this is an essential flavour in Thai cooking. Don't bother to buy the dried variety as it is pretty useless. Fresh is now generally available from most Asian food stores.

Gochu jang chilli paste This staple of Korean cooking is a thick, smooth bean paste laced with considerable quantities of chilli.

Hoisin sauce A thick, sweet, pungent sauce made from fermented soy beans, sugar, flour, vinegar, salt, garlic, chilli and sesame. In China, this is often used as a condiment with pork or duck.

Japanese pickled ginger Sushi's best friend, called *beni shoga*. Pickled slices of ginger are made by salting fresh ginger and marinating in rice vinegar and sugar.

Jellyfish Sold dried in plastic packs, it usually resembles an old, dry, car chamois. Soak for several hours and blanch in boiling water before using. The Chinese love to shred jellyfish, flavour it with vinegar and serve it in cold salads.

Kaffir limes Knobbly, misshapen limes native to Thailand. The rind is often used to flavour salads and stir fries, as are the glossy, double leaves, which are available fresh or frozen. Avoid the dried variety.

Kamaboko A rounded cake of fish paste, often coloured green or pink, and mostly sold frozen on little wooden boards. It is usually thawed, cut in thin slices and added to soups. Available from Japanese food stores.

Kecap manis A thick, sweet, dark soy sauce popular in Indonesian cooking.

Kimchi (Kimchee) This pungent, hot, fermented pickle, usually made with cabbage, is an essential accompaniment to just about any Korean dish you can think of. It is usually sold in plastic tubs or packets in the refrigerated section of Asian food stores. If you're lucky, you might even find it sold from the stone pot in which it was fermented.

Konbu Sea kelp, harvested from the cold waters of northern Japan. It is sold dried, in folded-up lengths, and is essential to the making of dashi.

Lemongrass A tall, lemon-scented spear-like grass used extensively in Thai and Malaysian cooking, both for fragrance and flavour. Usually, the outer leaves are removed and the white heart is sliced thinly before using. Buy fresh, if possible, and freeze any you don't use.

Lup cheong A hard, dry, sweet and salty Chinese sausage that looks like wrinkled up cabanossi. It is usually made from pork, but a darker variety is made with liver.

Menma Fermented pickled bamboo shoots. Available from Japanese food stores.

Mirin Sweet rice wine with a low alcohol content, used in Japanese cooking.

Miso A fermented paste of soybean, salt and either rice or barley. When mixed with dashi, it makes the popular Japanese miso soup.

Mushrooms, abalone Broad, pale, flat-gilled mushrooms, also known as oyster mushrooms. Readily available fresh.

Mushrooms, enoki Thin, white, needle-like mushrooms, available fresh.

Mushrooms, shiitake (or Chinese mushrooms) Flat, dark brown capped mushrooms popular in both China and Japan. Fresh shiitake are quite common these days, but they are more commonly bought in their dried form. When soaked, these have a pungent flavour and a firm chewiness.

Mushrooms, shimeji A Japanese variety that grows in grey, stumpy little clumps. Available fresh.

Nam pla ra The Thai name for a type of fish sauce made from freshwater mud fish. It is popular in Laos and northern Thailand. The pickled fish can be found in Thai groceries in jars under the name of pickled *gourami*. Boil it with 500 ml (16 fl oz) of water until fish disintegrates, then strain. See recipe on page 191.

Ngo gai (saw-leaf plant) A small, bright green plant with a distinctive saw-like leaf edge. It is sold fresh in most Vietnamese grocery stores.

Nori A seaweed, fried and pressed into sheets known as Asakusa nori. It is toasted lightly before using, either as a garnish or as the wrapping for rice rolls.

Nuoc cham A Vietnamese dipping sauce made by combining fish sauce (*nuoc mam*) with rice vinegar, garlic, water and sugar. See recipe on page 192.

Oyster sauce A dark, oyster-flavoured sauce thickened with cornflour and sold in bottles. These days, you will even find a vegetarian oyster sauce on the shelves of Chinese supermarkets.

Palm sugar A hard, dense sugar boiled down from palm sap. It has a treacle-like taste and is used extensively in Thai cooking.

Peanut oil The recipes specify peanut oil because I like peanut oil, but by all means use corn, canola, sunflower, safflower or any good, clean vegetable oil.

Potato starch A white flour made from potatoes and used as a thickener. Cornflour can usually be substituted.

Rau ram Sometimes called Vietnamese mint, although this long, slender, pointy, peppery leaf is not really a mint at all, but *Polygonum pulchrum*. As it is used to flavour laksa paste in Malaysia, it is also commonly called laksa leaf.

Red shallot A type of onion, smaller than the common brown or white onion. It has a mild, gentle flavour and dissolves more easily than others into sauces and stews when cooked. The more common brown shallot can be substituted.

Sake A clear wine 'brewed' from rice, with an alcohol content of about 16%. While it is often drunk warm from little pottery bottles, higher grades should always be served chilled.

Salted radish A dried, salted radish known as *hua pak gart kao* in Thailand. It is often sold as pale brown, moist shreds in packets labelled 'salted turnip'.

Sambal oelek see Chilli sambal

Sesame oil A dark, aromatic oil made from ground white sesame seeds. It is used more as a flavouring than a frying oil and is popular in northern China, Japan and Korea.

Sesame paste Asian sesame paste differs from Middle Eastern tahini in that it is made from toasted sesame seeds and not the untoasted variety. It is sold in jars in Chinese supermarkets. Smooth peanut butter can be used instead.

Shaohsing wine A strong-tasting Chinese rice wine predominantly used in cooking, rather than for drinking. Dry sherry makes a good substitute.

Shoei jeau pastry rounds Small, pale pastry rounds similar to wonton wrappers, although these are paler and a little thicker. They are used for making Korean Mandu dumplings and are readily available from Japanese and Korean groceries.

Shrimp paste see Belacan

Sichuan peppercorns The seed of the peppery ash tree (fagara), with a peppery, prickly flavour.

Sichuan preserved vegetable Mustard green roots preserved in salt and chilli and usually sold in cans.

Snake beans These are like string beans that couldn't stop growing. They are often sold in lengths of 50 cm (20 in) or more. They are particularly popular in Sichuan, where they are fried with pork and chilli.

Soy sauce, dark A heavier, darker soy sauce that, surprisingly, is lighter in salt.

Soy sauce, light A thinner, lighter soy that is fresh and salty.

Soy sauce, mushroom Soy sauce that has been flavoured with straw mushrooms.

Spring onions You might call them green onions, young green onions, scallions or even shallots, but as long as you mean the long green things with small barely formed white bulbs at the root ends, then we're talking about the same thing.

Star anise An attractive star-shaped spice with a striking, aniseed flavour.

Suckling pig Whole baby pig that is basted, then roasted over hot coals. It is the centrepiece of most Chinese celebrations and is revered for its crisp, red, roasted skin.

Tamarind A sour, citrus-like extract taken from the pods of tamarind trees and compressed into blocks. To make 1 cup tamarind water, mix 1 tablespoon tamarind pulp with 1 cup boiling water and let stand for 10 minutes before straining out the tamarind skin and seeds.

Tapioca starch A fine white power taken from the cassava root and used for thickening sauces. The same starch grains also form the tapioca balls that are favoured in desserts.

Taucheo see Brown bean sauce; yellow bean sauce

Tofu, fresh Cakes of freshly pressed bean curd, stored in water, and sold in packets of 6 cakes. Use quickly and change the water daily.

Tofu, hard A firm bean curd, made from soy beans and sold in vacuum packs in Oriental food stores.

Turmeric A rhizome of the ginger family. When dried, it provides the distinctive yellow colouring we have come to expect from Indian curry powder. Used fresh to flavour Thai curries and often eaten as a vegetable in its own right.

Vinegar, black A dark, pungent vinegar, usually made from glutinous rice, it is very popular in northern China. One of the best varieties is known as Chenkiang vinegar.

Vinegar, red A clear, pale, red rice vinegar, used mainly for dipping. It is the perfect accompaniment to shark fin and *wor tip*, or potsticker, dumplings.

Vinegar, rice A complex, pale vinegar made from fermented rice, and used widely in Japan, Korea and China.

Vinegar, white rice A mild, clear rice vinegar used in sweet-and-sour dishes.

Wakame A nutritious, dark seaweed usually sold in tiny, dried pieces. When soaked in tepid water for 15 minutes, it dramatically increases in size and is ready for use in soups or salads. Do not cook for more than a minute, as it will begin to lose its nutrients.

Wasabi Although it is often called Japanese horseradish, it is not related to European horseradish. Fresh wasabi root is almost impossible to find outside Japan, but it can be bought in powdered form in tins, or ready mixed in tubes.

Water chestnut The underwater corm of a type of watergrass, the water chestnut is a similar size to a regular chestnut, but has a papery skin and a deliciously crisp texture. It is occasionally found in its fresh form but is more usually available in cans, in pieces, slices, or shreds.

Water spinach Also called water convolvulus, this dark, leafy green has hollow stems and long pointy leaves. Known as *kangkong* in Malaysia and *ong choy* or *ung tsai* in China, it is often stir fried, or added to soups.

Wonton wrappers Looking like small, thin sheets of lasagne, these ready-made fresh dough sheets are used to make wonton dumplings and several yum cha dumplings.

Wood ear fungus Also known as black fungus and tree fungus, this glossy, rubbery fungus is prized for its crisp, crunchy texture. It is popular in stir fries and soups, and is mainly sold dried in plastic packets, although you may occasionally find it fresh.

Yellow bean sauce (taucheo) Another variant of Chinese bean sauce or brown bean sauce, this Malaysian type is also made by salting and fermenting yellow soy beans, but it is slightly paler and runnier. It is popular in fish dishes and noodle stir-fries. In Thailand, it is known as tao jiew, and is sold in tall, long-necked bottles.

Bibliography

Bharadwaj, Momisha, *The Indian Pantry*, Kyle Cathie Ltd., London, 1996.

Bhumichitr, Vatcharin, *The Taste of Thailand*, Pavilion Books, London, 1988.

Brennan, Jennifer, *Thai Cooking*, Futura, Great Britain, 1984.

Brissenden, Rosemary, *South East Asian Food*, Penguin, Melbourne, 1996.

Burum, Linda, *Asian Pasta*, Aris Books, California, 1985.

Chen, I-chow, *Szechuan Cooking*, Hilt Publishing Co., Taipei, 1994.

Choi, Trieu Thi and Isaak, Marcel, *The Food of Vietnam*, Periplus Editions, Hong Kong, 1997.

Chong, Elizabeth, *The Heritage of Chinese Cooking*, Weldon Russell, Sydney, 1993.

Dibbayawan, Pannipa, and Cox, Guy, *The Thai Cookbook*, Angus & Robertson, Sydney, 1988.

Downer, Lesley, and Yoneda, Minoru, *Step by Step Japanese Cooking*, Doubleday, Sydney, 1985.

Dupleix, Jill, *Malaysian*, Weidenfeld & Nicholson, London, 1997.

Dupleix, Jill, *New Food*, William Heinemann, Melbourne, 1994.

Fernandez, Rafi, *Malaysian Cookery*, Penguin, England, 1985.

Freeman, Meera, and Le Van Nhan, *The Vietnamese Cookbook*, Viking, Melbourne, 1995.

Goh, Simon, Durack, Terry, and Dupleix, Jill, *Hot Food Cool Jazz*, William Heinemann, Melbourne, 1993.

Hom, Ken, *Ken Hom's Chinese Cookery*, BBC, London, 1984.

Hsiung, Deh-Ta, *Chinese Regional Cooking*, Mayflower Books, New York, 1979.

Hutton, Wendy, *Singapore Food*, Ure Smith, Sydney, 1979.

Hutton, Wendy, *The Flavour of Malaysia*, Viking, Melbourne, 1994.

Hyun, Judy, *The Korean Cookbook*, Hollym, Chicago, 1970.

Kinsman, Lisa, *Chinese Delights*, William Collins, Sydney, 1982.

Krauss, Sven, Ganguillet, Laurent, Sanguanwong, Vira, and Warren, William, *The Food of Thailand*, Viking, Melbourne, 1994.

Kritikara, M. L. Taw, and Amranand, M.R. Pimsai, *Modern Thai Cooking*, Editions Duang Kamol, Bangkok, 1977.

Lee, Calvin B.T., and Evans, Audrey, *The Gourmet Chinese Regional Cookbook*, Castle, USA, 1976.

Lee, Y., *Thai Hawker Food*, Book Promotion & Service Ltd., Bangkok, 1993.

Leeming, Margaret and Huang, May Man-Hui, *Chinese Regional Cookery*, Rider, London, 1983.

Leeming, Margaret, and Huang, May Man-Hui, *Dim Sum*, Macdonald, London, 1985.

Lin, Florence, *Florence Lin's Complete Book of Chinese Noodles, Dumplings and Breads*, William Morrow, New York, 1986.

Lin, Hsiang, Ju and Tsuifeng, *Chinese Gastronomy*, Jill Norman & Hobhouse, London, 1982.

Lo, Kenneth, *Chinese Food*, Penguin, England, 1972.

Lo, Vivienne and Jenny, *150 Recipes from the Teahouse*, Faber & Faber, London, 1997.

Marks, Copeland, and Kim, Manjo, *The Korean Kitchen*, Chronicle Books, San Francisco, 1993.

McDermott, Nancie, *Real Thai*, Chronicle Books, San Francisco, 1992.

Morris, Sallie, *Oriental Cookery*, Doubleday, Sydney, 1984.

Morris, Sallie, *South East Asian Cookery*, Penguin, London, 1989.

Nartin, Peter and Joan, *Japanese Cooking*, Penguin, England, 1970.

Noriega, Violeta A., *Philippine recipes made easy*, Paperworks, Washington, 1993.

Passmore, Jacki, and Reid, Daniel P., *The Complete Chinese Cookbook*, Weldon, Sydney, 1982.

Passmore, Jacki, *The Encylopaedia of Asian Food and Cooking*, Doubleday, Sydney, 1991.

Perkins, David W., *Hong Kong & China Gas Chinese Cookbook*, The Hong Kong & China Gas Co., Hong Kong, 1978.

Routhier, Nicole, *Foods of Vietnam*, Stewart, Tabori & Chang, New York, 1989.

So, Yan-Kit, *Classic Food of China*, Macmillan, London, 1992.

Solomon, Charmaine, *Charmaine Solomon's Encyclopedia of Asian Food*, William Heinemann, Australia 1996.

Solomon, Charmaine, *The Complete Asian Cookbook*, Lansdowne Press, Sydney, 1976.

Stuart, Anh Thu, *Vietnamese Cooking*, Angus & Robertson, Sydney, 1986.

Thompson, David, *Classic Thai Cuisine*, Simon & Schuster, Sydney, 1993.

Tsuji, Shizuo, *Japanese Cooking: A Simple Art*, Kodansha International, New York, 1980.

Udesky, James, *The Book of Soba*, Kodansha International, Tokyo, 1988.

Index

This edition published in Great Britain in 1999 by
PAVILION BOOKS LIMITED
London House, Great Eastern Wharf
Parkgate Road, London SW11 4NQ

First published in Australia in 1998 by Allen & Unwin Pty Ltd

A CIP catalogue record for this book is available
from the British Library.

ISBN 1 86205 328 6

Printed in Hong Kong by South China Printing Co.

10 9 8 7 6 5 4 3 2 1

This book can be ordered direct from the publisher. Please contact
the Marketing Department. But try your bookshop first.